the FUNDRAISER who WANTED MORE

The five laws of persuasion that transform your results

the
FUNDRAISER
who WANTED
MORE

The **5** **laws**

of persuasion that
transform your results

Rob Woods

The Fundraiser Who Wanted More
The 5 laws of persuasion that transform your results

First paperback edition printed 2015 in the United Kingdom.

A catalogue record for this book is available from the British
Library.

ISBN 978-0-9932919-0-6

Published by Woods Training Limited
The Old Manse
High Street
Turvey
Bedfordshire
MK43 8DB

Designed by Bradbury and Williams

This book is dedicated to Wilf and May,
the best influencers I know

About the Author

Award-winning trainer Rob Woods has worked in fundraising since January 2000. Originally a fundraiser for the NSPCC, since becoming an independent trainer and coach in 2007 he has helped more than five thousand fundraisers and directors, chief executives and trustees.

Rob has helped organisations of every size, from small charities with little dedicated fundraising resource, to some of the world's leading charitable organisations. His clients include Cambridge University, CRUK, Oxfam, Macmillan Cancer Care, and The British Heart Foundation. He is a tutor for the Institute of Fundraising Academy.

What others have said about this book

'I've always found Rob's courses immensely helpful for my fundraising teams, and this book is full of the shrewd insight that you get from those sessions. If you want your team to be more confident, proactive and persuasive, let them read this book.'

ANDY HARRIS, DIRECTOR OF FUNDRAISING AND COMMUNICATIONS, *BREAST CANCER CARE*

'I lead a team of fundraisers, so I know the many things that can make our job difficult. This book is refreshingly different because not only is it highly readable, it also provides clear steps for how you can become more successful when talking to your donors. If you want to secure more gifts for your charity, read this book.'

CHARLOTTE WHITE, HEAD OF INDIVIDUAL GIVING, *NATIONAL TRUST*

'The strategies I learned on Rob's training programme helped my team and I raise new gifts worth more than £200,000. This book brings many of those techniques to life. As always with Rob, he not only helps you to set out the steps needed to make lots of money for your charity, but also helps you understand how you can implement those steps on a daily basis.'

PAUL MCKENZIE, HEAD OF MAJOR GIVING AND PARTNERSHIPS, *BATTERSEA DOGS AND CATS HOME*

"Having Rob in the room for a day of training can transform the way you feel about your role and how you are able to make your charity's needs come to life to donors. But you can't have Rob with you face to face every day. This book is the next best thing. It's filled with the wisdom, humanity and hope that Rob offers at his events. I challenge anyone not to be a better fundraiser if they read this and follow even just one of the key tips."

MARK BISHOP, DIRECTOR OF FUNDRAISING, *PROSTATE CANCER UK*

Acknowledgments

I'd like to say a huge thank you to the many people who have shared their ideas and advice to help me shape this book, including: Katie Macdonald, Heidi Lagumina, Charlotte White, Jonathan Andrews, Ciaran Biggins, Carla Cornwell, Kim van Niekerk, Lucy Gower, Rich Lennon, Chris Martinez, Roy Williams and Ken Burnett.

A special thank you to Katy Taberham and Sarah Pugh for your ideas and powerful stories.

Thanks to Poppy, Wilf and May for all your encouragement and support.

Contents

When less really is more
Foreword from Ken Burnett

Simple, we are often reminded, doesn't equal easy. And that which is written with ease is usually read with difficulty. Yet despite the obvious attractiveness of simplicity most people prefer to dress up the points they want to make, to obscure their meaning with organisation-speak, to wrap their ideas in jargon and acronyms in the hope that they'll seem more important and learned. Writers of reports and fundraisers seem particularly prone to this affliction. Yet more seldom means better in business writing.

Which is why I'm happy to be commending this book. Effective communication is the core of great fundraising, so mastery of it is essential for serious fundraisers. The five big ideas that Rob Woods wants us to understand and act on in this short, easily accessible text are the more so because he's kept his messages simple, uncluttered and sharply focused. In doing so he's given us a guide that's usable as well as useful, easy to read and digest in one or two sittings. In short, it's delightful.

Don't be fooled by Rob's simple style, for it demands real mastery of the subjects and fluency of expression too if it's to pave the way for these career-changing insights. This simplicity helps us to quickly appreciate that these big ideas are based on deep understanding matched by easy familiarity and a confidence borne of practice and direct experience.

It's a short book too. George Bernard Shaw famously apologised to his readers for writing a long letter, explaining that he didn't have time (and perhaps energy or interest) to write a shorter one. He knew what he was talking about. Saying something important in few words is a skill that few master, though most readers relish it.

So its brevity and ease of understanding should all recommend this slender tome to you. But important and appreciated though these attributes are, the real value in these words and pages, I'm sure, is their content. What Rob Woods says here is profoundly right and very helpful for the determined, ambitious fundraiser. I hope you will enjoy this book and profit from it too.

Ken Burnett
March 2015

Introduction

I have written this book for anyone who has ever found fundraising difficult and wished there was an easier way.

When I first became a professional fundraiser I found it more challenging than I had expected. I should not have been surprised – most disciplines worth pursuing involve more skill and diligent practice than are obvious from the outside. When I was struggling I tried various things, but the one that helped me most was to look for people who were consistently getting great results and ask them how they did it.

Admittedly not all of the high achievers I interviewed were able to explain their techniques. But from most of these conversations I took away useful insights and distinctions that would have taken me years of trial and error to work out for myself.

By modelling these proven techniques I started to make progress in my own job. Since then I have met dozens of high-achieving fundraising professionals and found out precisely how they get their results. I've used these patterns to design practical tools to help any fundraiser, from any type or size of charity, to raise more money.

Over the years I have had the privilege of delivering training programmes for some of the most successful charities, arts organisations and universities in the world, including Save the Children and UNICEF, The Dragon School and Tate, Oxford and Cambridge Universities.

Last week I was excited to hear from a client who had just closed the deal on a long term corporate partnership worth more than £5 million for his charity. Influencing the company to raise its sights and develop a truly ground-breaking partnership, he applied all five of the principles that I explore in this book. Two weeks ago I heard from another client that these same influencing techniques worked so well in a pitch that the company phoned her two hours after her presentation. They were so keen to choose her charity that they cancelled the next stage of their process, the staff vote. The partnership is worth £250,000.

I'm not saying this to impress you. I'm saying it to impress upon you that when you find out what very successful people do and you find ways to do the same things, you can achieve extraordinary results. If you have ever wanted to raise more and to give more, to enjoy your job more and to become more, I want you to know that all these things are possible. And I hope you find this book a valuable tool for the journey.

Rob Woods

CHAPTER 1

The **FIRST** law

'Please do fill out your evaluation forms before you leave – feel free to tick excellent as much as you like ... and have a good lunch.' And with that the tall, sharp-suited man finished his presentation, flashed his winning smile and strolled off the stage. He looked extremely pleased.

Sitting on the end of a row near the back, Claire grabbed a form from the chair next to her. She ticked boxes at speed and made for the door. After a dispiriting morning at the UK Conference for Fundraising, she was determined to avoid having to wait hours to get lunch.

In the vast lunch room and exhibition centre she joined the shortest queue she could find. The place was already busy and around her the other delegates were chatting, but Claire wasn't in the mood for small talk with people she'd never meet again.

The heavy feeling in her chest had not gone away. If anything, during the last presentation, she'd become more despondent than ever.

Behind one of the recruitment stands she found a free table and sat down with her fish and salad.

'May I join you?'

Claire looked up and nodded at the middle-aged man. The place was so busy that she'd known she'd have to share her table with someone, but still, she craved a few minutes' peace. She hoped he wouldn't be in the mood to chat either.

'My name's Mark.'

'Hi Mark. Claire,' she said, shaking the hand he'd offered.

'How was your morning?' he asked.

'Pretty rubbish,' she said flatly. She'd surprised herself with her bluntness.

But then, something about the smugness of the speaker in the final session, Hugo Someone-or-Other, had been the last straw. Working for some famous international children's charity – not exactly Mission Impossible – he'd told them how much money he'd raised no less than four times. And he'd told them about the system called the *seven steps of donor solicitation* as if it was the answer to every problem a fundraiser could ever experience.

Above all, he exhorted them all to get out and be more *brave* and just go and *talk* to donors and companies. And yet in sixty minutes she had not heard a single practical idea that she could apply to her own fundraising challenges. 'Just do it' seemed to be the sum total of his message, indeed, one of his slides had said precisely that. She had even plucked up the courage to ask him to be more specific as to what she should say to a company or donor. His answer had been that 'The most important thing you've got to do is speak with *passion*'.

'Oh, passion. Well, I'll just go and do that shall I?' she had found herself scribbling angrily in her notebook.

'I'm sorry to hear that. Do you want to tell me about it?'

The stranger had interrupted Claire's reverie. It was a bit disarming, but his tone was unusually genuine. She got the impression that he was actually interested.

And so Claire found herself telling him how the three sessions she'd attended had left her more depressed than ever. It wasn't so much that she didn't believe the speakers were good at their jobs – it was just that to sit through three, hour-long sessions and take away nothing practical that she could go and do left her facing the conclusion that the problem must be with her, not the speakers.

Plenty of people around her had been diligently taking notes. And most of the room now seemed buzzing with energy and presumably, inspiration. And she felt flat. Flat, and with a heavy ache in her chest as she faced the realisation that the world of fundraising and charities probably wasn't for her after all.

And throughout all of this, her lunch companion had not interrupted her, not tried to cheer her up, and not told her what she should be feeling. He really had simply listened in the purest sense of the word. And she found that feeling listened to, or more to the point, feeling actually *understood*, was a good feeling.

Before long, she'd said all she wanted to say about the conference but felt the need to ask Mark's opinion.

'The problem I've got is that I'm really struggling at work, and all last week I had built up in my mind that if I could just get some good ideas at this conference, I could go back and try to turn things around. Now I'm wondering if I'm even cut out to do fundraising at all ...'

'Would you like my opinion?'

'You know, I think I would. Tell me.'

'Is this the first conference about fundraising you've been to?'

She nodded.

'Well then,' he said, and paused, as if that explained everything.

Then he carried on, 'I really like these conferences. They do a lot of good. In fact, they change the world. But, like many things in life, there's a knack to getting the most from them. And just as Christmas can be lonely and depressing, precisely because it sometimes fails to live up to what you hoped for and because of how happy everyone else seems to be, so a conference presentation can be a very frustrating sixty minutes of your life, if you find yourself in a session that doesn't serve you.

'The great thing about a conference this size is that it has so many sessions, that people who've not given many presentations before can come and share their ideas. Without this, the charity sector would go stale. It's vital that there are always new ideas and strategies being shared. And it's vital that the leaders of the future get a chance to come and do that sharing, and indeed become better speakers and leaders in the process.

'Having said all that ... the great challenge is that, the first time you attend, unless you get good advice from someone who's experienced at seeing through the promise of a flash presentation title and description, it's in the lap of the gods whether the sessions you go to are any use to you. And the reason you've had a rubbish morning is that you're incorrectly interpreting the speaker's inexperience as evidence that you don't have what it takes to succeed as a fundraiser.'

'But all the speakers I heard speak were experienced. The last guy,

Hugo Smug had been doing it for sixteen years, which he told us no fewer than six times.'

'As fundraisers, yes. And I bet they're good at their jobs as fundraisers, even, quite possibly, the one who was so full of clichés but short on practical examples. But taking a story of something you've done well as a fundraiser and delivering it as a conference session that holds the audience's interest and is genuinely useful to all of them, is much harder than most people realise. Don't underestimate the level of skill and practice you need to do it well. And this is even before we take into account the great variety in the levels of experience, interests and learning styles of the people in the audience. Some of the presentations this morning could have been really good, but just not the right session for what you need at the moment.'

Most of this resonated with what Claire had known at some subconscious level, but had not been able to articulate with any confidence. As Mark offered a new meaning for what had happened that morning, she was sure he was right because the heavy feeling in her chest had lightened a little.

Relieved, she thanked him. And he said that as he'd been coming to these conferences for years, he'd be happy to help her work out which sessions that afternoon might be most useful to her.

'But you mentioned that you've been finding things difficult at work recently. May I ask what you're not enjoying?'

The sinking feeling returned. 'Well, it's just that after all this time I still haven't managed to raise much money. I'm not afraid of pressure or even hard work – I worked in recruitment for seven years for goodness sake – but I never thought fundraising would be quite *this* hard.'

'How long have you been doing it?'

'I joined eight months ago, and this is my first fundraising job, although I did some things for rag when I was at uni.'

'So you feel you haven't managed to make it work yet?'

'That's right. I'm supposed to split my time between major gifts and corporate partnerships, but our charity is so small that there are always plenty of other things to do as well. I've been working hours at least as long as when I was in the commercial sector, longer probably when you add in the evening events … and yet I still can't seem to raise anywhere near the financial target I've been set.

'And I'm actually not so bad at it. I mean, I think I've got more of a clue than some of my colleagues. It's just that I hate the feeling of muddling through. When I was at school I wasn't top of the class but there were things I knew I was good at. There were things I could get good marks in. But it's not just the results … although I do miss that feeling of winning sometimes, but it's more than that. I think I also just miss that feeling of knowing what I'm doing, you know.'

Mark nodded. 'Yes, to feel that confident, winning feeling, even just occasionally, is really important I think.'

Claire looked at Mark.

'I guess I just want more. Not more in the sense of more salary – although at some point that would be nice – so much as in the sense of getting better at what I do, and being able to make a bigger difference. Many of the families who use Alice House are really struggling anyway, let alone the pain they go through when their loved one has cancer or Parkinson's disease or whatever. I wanted to work for a charity because I wanted to do more, become more, above all, be able to help more people who're in trouble. I really had this sense that this was for me. And over the last few months the reason I've been getting depressed is that I've realised that it hasn't worked out.'

> 'I guess I just want more. Not more in the sense of more salary – although at some point that would be nice – so much as in the sense of getting better at what I do, and being able to make a bigger difference.'

'Hmm. I see that would feel depressing.' Mark chewed his bread roll.

'And which part of your job do you find you're doing pretty well at?' he asked.

She looked blankly at him.

'And before your brain says *none of it*, listen to me because this is important. When we get stressed our state changes for the worse. The more lousy our state the less we notice all the things that are actually going pretty well or that we *could* be pleased about. And the more that happens, the less likely we are to think straight about the thing that is genuinely not going well and needs sorting out.'

Claire nodded. She was aware that over the last few weeks some difficult issues at work had affected her mind-set outside work too. But what could she do about it?

'So,' Mark continued, 'when this happens to me one thing I do is I force myself, or someone else helps me, to focus on what's going well or, for instance I could be grateful for. There are *always* bright spots if you're determined enough to find them. So, which bits of your job have been going well or at least going okay?'

Claire's mind was blank and, frankly, the question was annoying. If she'd wanted some 'positive thinking' pep talk she'd have asked for it. 'I honestly don't know. I suppose there may be some things ... but I don't know.'

'Sure, I see that.' And then still smiling, unfazed by the irritation in her voice, he playfully added, 'But, if you *did* know, what would you say you've been doing at least quite well?'

'Well, I guess ... my manager has said I'm pretty good on the phone,' she admitted.

'Oh, is that all?' he said, in mock disappointment. 'You're good on the phone?'

'Yeah, well, we're all supposed to make a certain number of calls to companies who've helped us in the past and potential major donors from our database to try and get a meeting with them to see if they want to get involved again ... and because in recruitment you've got no choice but to get good on the phone ... I've found that part of the job isn't too hard for me.'

Mark was grinning. 'Do you know how many fundraisers I know who struggle at the thing you're good at?'

He was making a good point. Claire did know. Many of her colleagues found securing meetings with prospective supporters really hard. She felt a bit silly to have completely ignored the thing she did actually know she was pretty good at. Which was also annoying. And yet she admitted to herself that somehow to realise it did make her feel a bit better.

'So, assuming there are some other things you're doing okay at, what do you think is getting in the way of your results?'

She knew the answer to this one, as she'd known since her very first meeting with a potential donor. 'Getting the meetings with these wealthy or corporate people isn't always easy, but it's true that I've been doing okay at it. The problem is what happens when I get there.'

'What do you mean?'

'Well, it's usually not awful ... I mean, we have a conversation, it's just that it rarely goes anywhere. Sometimes they tell me to my face that they can't help because their budgets have been cut, or they won't have a bonus this year, or whatever. And sometimes they seem quite interested and so I go and write a proposal or go back and find out some information – which is often a lot of work ... and then they go quiet. It's as if they were never really interested in the first place.'

'Don't you just hate that? So annoying ... and it can happen all too easily. Why do you think it happens?'

'I used to think it was the donors' fault ... that they're mean, or at least usually really fickle. Now I think I've realised it's probably just that I'm no good at it. This morning I'd concluded that I don't have the talent you need to succeed as a relationship fundraiser.'

Mark laughed, 'You don't have what it takes, eh?' This gave her a jolt. The other people she'd confided this painful realisation to had been more sympathetic.

'What's funny?'

'Forgive me', he said, 'it's just that I've heard that one a lot and it's very rarely true. But I shouldn't laugh. When I was struggling in my first fundraising job I made the same false conclusion.'

'So what happened to change your mind?'

'Well, luckily I got advice from someone who was both experienced and successful. What she told me – what I'm about to tell you – is probably the most important idea in successful fundraising. In fact, it translates across into success in anything.

'People who consistently raise more money than you,' he explained, 'are not more talented than you. They're not even luckier than you. They are simply thinking different thoughts and doing different things.'

Claire was confused. 'Isn't that the same thing?'

'Not exactly. Look at it this way. If you believe that some people are talented and some are not, you shut down the possibility that any of us can ever achieve great results. But if you see their success in terms of them thinking and doing different things it follows that anyone who wants those results simply has to learn, and often simply choose, to model those same ways of thinking and acting.'

At some level it made sense, but at another it was nonsense. 'It sounds like you're saying there's no such thing as talent. Of course there is *talent*. Whatever you tell me, I can never accept that I could …' she paused, searching for an example, 'I can never accept that I could win an Olympic medal for the 100 metres or, say, compose a concerto.'

Mark chuckled. 'I agree that everyone is born different. I think we're born with a unique combination of interests and even predispositions to be good at the things we are drawn to, and some of those often become strengths, especially if we're in an environment that rewards those strengths. And it may be that growing up, you were not drawn to sprinting or composing. But here's my point – if right now, you're in the right kind of job, that is, the job you feel fits your purpose in life, then there is no skill you can't dramatically improve if you set your mind to it.'

Mark paused, and Claire weighed up this last sentence. She decided it made sense, at least in theory.

'The most important question for you to ask is not "Am I right for fundraising?" but rather, "Is fundraising right for me?" The decisive factor is not about how skilful you currently are. What matters is "Do you *want* to be a fundraiser?"' Mark paused for a moment. 'Well, do you?'

In her heart Claire knew the answer was a 'YES'. The very reason she'd felt so despondent lately was that her dream of a successful career making a difference in the charity sector – something she'd nurtured for years, especially through the toughest times in her old job – was crumbling to dust.

'Yes. Of course I want to work in fundraising. I've wanted to get into the charity sector and make a difference for at least five years… but I'm still not sure if I'm any good at it.'

'That's where I may be able to help. I've been working with charities for many years now and I know what brings results. When someone is clear they want to do this job, and do it to the best of their ability, there are plenty of things they can do to improve the most important skills. And so can you.'

'You make it sound simple.'

> '...if right now, you're in the right kind of job, that is, the job you feel fits your purpose in life, then there is no skill you can't dramatically improve if you set your mind to it.'

'Well yes, like lots of things it is simple, in theory. It's just not always *easy*, if you can see the difference. If it was easy, all 700 people in this room would be fulfilling their massive potential. And my guess is that though some are, many are not. There is just one thing that means that most people never do what is needed to make consistent improvement in the key skills of fundraising.'

'What's the thing?'

'Decision. They haven't decided. They never get utterly certain that they're going to do what it takes to become outstanding in this field.'

Mark looked her in the eye.

'This is what I call "the first law". In fundraising, as in life, all great progress starts with a decision.'

The first law – the law of decision
'In fundraising, as in life, all great progress starts with a decision.'

'The truth is that there are no skills in fundraising which can't be dramatically improved if you set your mind on it. You can, and you will, be exactly as successful as you decide to be. The person who has taught me most about how to make deliberate progress, how to be both successful and fulfilled, is the author and speaker, Tony Robbins. He suggests that life will give you whatever you want in terms of success, if you get truly clear that that is what you are aiming for. Most people get a bit better through time. If you want to make extraordinary progress you can do that too ... *but only if you decide to.*

'Believe me, if you don't decide, you'll never take advantage of all the opportunities available to you. You'll never raise your standards and hold yourself to those standards. You'll never follow up and do what's needed when the going gets tough. But if you do decide, I've seen with my own eyes again and again that extraordinary things are possible.'

Mark's tone had become intense. Claire couldn't help but look away to try and process what he was saying. The room was beginning to empty of people. She looked back at Mark. 'Is that it? I just make a decision?'

'That's it.'

'I can do that,' she said.

Mark smiled. His eyes were twinkling. 'Great! The key is not to worry about the gap between where you are now and where you want to be. This is so, so important. You must believe this, or it's really hard to make the decision in your heart. Trust that there are ways to get there and, if you search for them, you will find them.'

She nodded. 'Okay. I don't really know where to start, but for now I won't let that get in the way of my decision.'

'That's it. I've got two more things to say. Firstly, if you're serious about this decision, write it down as soon as possible. Whenever I write things down I become much more likely to follow through on them.'

> 'Trust that there are ways to get there and, if you search for them, you will find them.'

'Okay. And the other thing?'

'If you'd like, we could have a quick look at what conference sessions are on this afternoon and I can offer my thoughts on which are most likely to make up for your bad luck this morning.'

It took five minutes. Together they worked out the sessions most likely to provide Claire with what she was looking for. Then, with four minutes left before the afternoon session started, she thanked Mark, shook his hand and hurried back towards the seminar rooms.

Claire had a lot to think about as she travelled home that evening. She used her travel time to flick through the notes she'd made that afternoon, which had indeed been a vast improvement on her morning. Flicking through the speaker profiles at the back of the brochure, she also noticed that Mark was one of the speakers. His biography made for impressive reading and she tried to work out why she found this surprising. Of course, there is no reason why someone successful should not be helpful to a complete stranger at a conference. If you were successful you probably would be friendly, wouldn't you?

Sitting on the top level of the W3 bus, she pulled out the conference notebook and a pen. Opening a fresh page, she wrote these words:

I, Claire Hardie, have decided to become an outstanding fundraiser.

It felt weird for someone who was truly struggling in their job to write such nonsense. But there was a truth running through the conversation she'd had with Mark that had struck a chord with her. One of the things which made complete sense to her was that 'there are no skills in fundraising which can't be dramatically improved if you set your mind on it'.

Claire also found it strangely empowering that right now she had nothing much to lose. So, amused at herself, she wrote a second sentence.

And I'm fully committed to making this happen (even if I don't know what to do yet).

• THE FIRST LAW •
THE LAW OF
DECISION

—

IN FUNDRAISING,
AS IN LIFE,
ALL GREAT PROGRESS
STARTS WITH
A DECISION

—

CHAPTER 2

The road less travelled

The next day Claire did something she would not normally have done. When her colleague Andy said he wasn't able to use his ticket to the third day of the conference she asked if she could go in his place. She decided to go in spite of all the things on her to do list. Surprisingly, no one else had put up a fight for the ticket. They'd all been too busy.

Earlier that morning she'd done something equally out of character. When on the tube she'd noticed a young woman holding one of the distinctive orange conference bags, Claire asked to sit down beside her and struck up a conversation about what sessions she planned to go to that day.

As it turned out, the other fundraiser had been coming to this conference for several years and knew many of the speakers. She suggested some sessions she felt Claire would find useful.

And Claire was delighted to discover that her bravery was paying off. Her day so far had been infinitely more encouraging than the previous morning. She'd written down several ideas that she knew would help her in her job. And, just as importantly, the speakers this morning had not acted as though everything was easy. She felt that they understood her challenges. But their stories and above all their manner had further strengthened her sense that Mark was right. If you search for them there are dozens of things you can do to improve your knowledge and skills and so make your job easier.

Then she saw Mark at one of the lunch tables. Although she wanted to go and say hello, she hesitated. 'Just because he was friendly before, it doesn't give me the right to barge right up to him,' she told herself. Then she remembered one of the ideas that had struck a chord with her that morning. She'd left a fantastic session about networking inspired by the extraordinary power of making it your habit to talk to people you don't know. The speaker had said, 'If you see someone you'd like to speak to, seize the day. Move to go and talk to them within three seconds, before the little voice in your head can talk you out of it.' The accompanying slide had stuck in her head:

She who hesitates ... waits and waits and waits

It had reminded her of a couple of the sadder 'nearly' moments in her life when she had waited for the perfect timing, or the perfect words, or the perfect feeling of confidence, to go and talk to someone only to discover that the moment slipped away.

'Not this time,' she decided. As the networking speaker had advised, she walked confidently towards Mark, and waited patiently but not 'playing low and humble'.

He was chatting merrily with someone he seemed to know quite well, but when there was a natural pause in the conversation he noticed Claire and grinned broadly, 'Claire, hello again.'

Excusing himself from the woman he stepped towards Claire and said 'How about coffee?'

'I'd like that. I didn't want to interrupt but I wanted to thank you for your help yesterday.'

Over coffee, she told him about writing her decision to commit to becoming an outstanding fundraiser in her conference notebook. 'Strange as it sounds, it already seems to be helping.' She explained how she'd started acting more boldly by asking for Andy's conference ticket and introducing herself to the stranger on the tube, and how she'd been paid back through a really inspiring morning.

'I'm so pleased you're having a much better day. And it's not really strange is it?' said Mark smiling. 'As soon as someone makes a decision and genuinely commits, various things get easier.'

'Yes, I think I believe that now. But there is something else I wanted to ask you. Now that I have a sense of what's possible, I want to learn as much as I can, as quickly as I can. I feel better now, but the pressure at work hasn't gone away. I wondered if you'd help me work out how to go about improving my fundraising skills.'

'I'd like to help you Claire, and I'll tell you why. You heard something which you thought might help you and you found the courage to actually follow through.' His face became serious. 'I've worked with thousands of fundraisers over the years. Do you know how few people actually do exactly what they said they were going to do? Surprisingly few. In this chaotic world there will always be reasons not to. Most people think that success is achieved through the big moments. The big £1 million pitches or the rare interview chances. In fact success is largely driven by simply following through on the many small-seeming things day in, day out. These compound to shape habits. Habits create character. This kind of character not only increases your self-respect, but it leads to massive success.

'Most people don't do what they said they would do. You were probably feeling tired and discouraged. Yet you still did what you said you would do.'

Claire nodded. She *had* been tired and it would have been so easy to not quite put pen to paper.

'Claire, I can sense that you're serious about making the most of your career, so I'd like to help. I'd be happy to meet you four more times. At each of those meetings I'll share with you one of the remaining five laws of persuasive fundraising conversations.'

'The five laws of persuasive fundraising conversations?' Claire repeated. She was intrigued. 'In what sense are they laws?'

'...success is largely driven by simply following through on the many small-seeming things day in, day out.'

'Well, they're not laws in the sense that if you do these five things everyone will give you money every time. That would be impossible because obviously the decision to make a donation or for a company to form a partnership will never be yours. A good fundraiser can make it easier for someone to want to give for *their* reasons, but that decision must (and thankfully, does) always rest with them. So, the laws

THE FUNDRAISER WHO WANTED MORE

don't guarantee income every time, nor will you be punished for not following them, but they do maximise the chances that people who could care about your kind of charity will feel motivated to help. And if you have enough meetings with the right people and companies, the laws will absolutely lead to fantastic income for your charity.'

Claire nodded. What he said made enough sense for her to want to at least hear what the laws were, so she could judge for herself.

Mark continued, 'But there's one condition and it's this: you must go and apply the principle immediately. If you don't, our agreement will be terminated.'

Two thoughts struck Claire … What an opportunity! And what a weird condition! She wanted to know what he meant by *immediately*.

'It means you need to take some action to apply that particular law that same week, at the very least, and ideally that same day. Make a phone call, order a book, mentally rehearse how you'll apply the idea with your next donor – anything that builds momentum and gives you the opportunity of doing the law, rather than merely evaluating it *theoretically*.'

While that all sounded good, and she truly wanted to agree, the reality of her chaotic work environment was weighing on her mind.

Mark smiled. 'I understand why you'd hesitate. You're thinking of the endless stream of emails and all the extra things you're asked to do that keep you from following through on your "to do" list. You're already busy without new things to follow up on from me.'

Claire nodded. After asking for Andy's ticket yesterday she'd had to be extremely disciplined in order to get through the most urgent things she had to do.

'Following through and changing a habit

'…unless you commit now that you're going to test the five laws by taking action, they will be pretty useless and we'll have both wasted our time.'

is usually harder to do in practice than it sounds.' Mark continued. 'There are psychological reasons why it's much easier to carry on as you were before. So unless you commit now that you're going to test the five laws by taking action, they will be pretty useless and we'll have both wasted our time.'

Claire nodded. 'That makes sense to me. Its only worth doing if I'm going to actually follow through, so I agree to your condition. I will take action on the same day as our meeting and if that's just not possible then at the very latest I'll always follow through within the same week,' she said, smiling.

Although the melodrama that Mark introduced was odd, Claire knew that anything that made her more likely to follow through was in her interests.

'So tell me, when do we start?'

'Next week.'

CHAPTER 3

The **SECOND** law

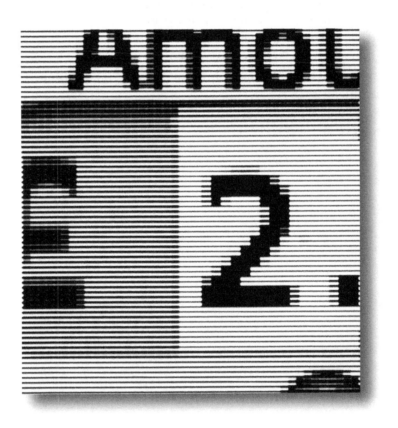

A few days after the conference, Claire received an email from Mark inviting her to a meeting with his friend Freya at the North London Dogs Home in Bounds Green.

Claire arrived at the charity's offices at 12.30 and was relieved to find Mark sitting in the reception area, reading a paperback. While she was signing the visitor's book, the receptionist called Freya.

Soon a door opened and in strode a cheerful-looking woman who walked straight to Mark and kissed him on the cheek.

'Mark, how *are* you?'

After a quick exchange of greetings, Mark turned to Claire. 'Claire, this is Freya. She's going to show us round.'

'Hello Claire, I'm so pleased to meet you. Let's go and have some tea.' Freya led them into the kitchen, which was a large, light room with a wooden table and a dozen chairs.

While the kettle was boiling, Mark told Freya that he was helping Claire with her fundraising, and he thought she'd be ideally placed to show her the second law.

'Ahh, the second law ... happily, I will tell you about the second law of persuasive fundraising conversations but to be honest, I can only really help you once I know a bit more about you. Would you like to tell me about your fundraising job so far?'

Claire told Freya some of what she had told Mark the previous week, about what an extraordinary place the Alice House Hospice was to work, and about what she had been finding difficult in her first fundraising job. Freya and Mark said very little but within a minute or two, Claire felt strangely at ease talking to Freya. She didn't notice to begin with but as she found herself talking more and more freely, she realised it was because Freya was truly interested in what Claire had to say. In fact, she felt so understood that she even heard herself explaining things in ways that she had not done before, almost as if she was thinking out loud.

Claire found herself telling Freya about a meeting with a partner of a local estate agent which had not gone well.

'How do you mean, it didn't go well?'

'Well, it wasn't a disaster; it's just that he didn't seem that interested.'

'And can you remember what you said?'

'Well, sure, I did what my manager always used to do. You know, I laid out what the hospice is, what sort of patients come to stay, the various ways we help them.'

'Okay, and how long do you think this took?'

'Well, not long, maybe five or ten minutes. I could tell he wasn't interested, but what else could I do? He started the meeting by asking me to give him a bit of background to the charity.'

'I'm sure he did, but what I've found is that although potential supporters often do need some information about the charity, at the start of the conversation they tend to need far less than we think. So by all means, be able to state what your charity does, but make sure it's very brief. This is one of those situations when less counts for more.'

'But why? If the donor asks you a question, shouldn't you answer it?'

'Absolutely, you should answer it but, if you really care about helping that person to enjoy and be interested in what you have to say, then it's really important that you shouldn't say too much before you've got to know them a bit. The second law states that you can best influence someone if you have first understood and appreciated their world.

The second law – the law of understanding
'If you want to influence someone, first understand and appreciate their world.'

'Said differently, this is the 'law of saying as little as possible till you've understood as much as you can about the other person.'

'Okay, that makes sense – so you need an elevator pitch?'

Mark twitched his head slightly to one side. Freya smiled.

'Mark and I tend not to use that phrase, because to us it gives the impression that you should be able to say something brief, when talking to someone you barely know, that is designed to get the other person to want to support you. And near the start of a conversation, we have not found it is possible or necessarily desirable to aim to "pitch" anything to them. To us, "pitching" sounds too forward, and could cause a fundraiser to destroy what little rapport they may have achieved that early in the conversation.'

'Well okay, I guess that makes sense. So it's not a pitch. So what do you say then?'

'Good question, which I'll answer in a minute. And an even more important question is not what do you say, but why do you say it?'

'Why? Well, because they asked you.'

'Well yes, they did ask you. But my main objective in answering is not to tell them everything, but to find a way to help them want to tell me some things early on. Because it's not possible to really give a proper explanation of just how amazing your charity is until you have understood even some basic things about the other person.

'So what I do is make sure I've memorised a short answer to the question "what does your charity do?", and I tend to stick to that because otherwise I've found it's all too easy to give far too much detail about things they may not be interested in.'

'So you're saying I should only go into detail once I know more about them, in the same way that any good salesperson cannot help a

> '**Because it's not possible to really give a proper explanation of just how amazing your charity is until you have understood even some basic things about the other person.**'

customer until they've understood some of their needs and wants?'

'That's right. Now I had always known this in theory, it's just that in my first couple of years doing this job, however much I intended not to say too much till I had understood the would-be supporter, I would end up inadvertently talking too much. It's not hard to do.'

'Yes, I see how that could happen,' Claire said ruefully. 'But what about research? With the companies I'm talking to, I'm finding out whatever I can on-line long before the meeting stage in the relationship. And come to think of it, with quite a lot of our major supporters and trusts, we ought to know a quite a bit about who they are before we arrive. What does the law of understanding say about that?'

'It says that if you're invited to a formal pitch, by which I mean they want you to respond to a written brief and present to a panel ... in those cases, you have to gather your insight in advance of the pitch. And in the context of corporate fundraising, the law of understanding suggests that whichever fundraiser worked harder and more creatively to truly understand the actual reasons why the members of the panel would say 'yes', has the edge in creating a winning pitch. But even in corporate fundraising, the pitch is not the most common format for persuading people to support you.

'In corporate, community, event and major donor fundraising, by all means do as much research as you can before you meet them ... but still the most effective meeting strategy should be to help the other person want to talk to you early on. I appreciate that doing this in practice is easier with some donors than with others but still, it should be what we intend to have happen early in the meeting, every time. Because, when you think about it, we can't help someone at a deep level, before we've understood them.'

'And what about supporters you've met before and know well?'

'Good question. Yes, I even carry out the same idea with donors I know really well. Obviously, I'm not going to go over the summary of the charity again, but I am going to resist the urge to dive into any detail about whatever proposal or new fundraising idea I want to discuss, until I've helped them talk to me, so I can tune into and appreciate their world. Everyone sees and internally represents things slightly differently. The better I understand those things, the more easily I can choose what to say and how to say it, in line with both what they care about and how they like to communicate.'

'Okay, so can you give me an example?'

'Well, what I say for the North London Dogs Home is something like "Because far too many dogs are mistreated and abandoned, what we do is take care of them until we can find them a safe and loving home with a new family."'

Claire nodded.

'You see, it's not exciting or clever-sounding and it usually doesn't include a statistic. It's a just a sensible and very brief explanation, in everyday language. So what could you say?'

'Errrr ... well I don't know ... I guess ... "Alice House is a hospice that takes care of people with life-limiting diseases, so that they can live as full a life as possible while they are alive, and when the time comes to die, they can do so with comfort and company and dignity."'

'Sounds good to me,' said Mark.

'That'll do fine,' agreed Freya.

Claire looked surprised. 'But there's so much I haven't said. What about our day centre and our hospice at home support and ... and our emphasis on the needs of the family as well as the patient. I'd been led to believe these are all essential things I have to make people aware of.'

'I imagine they are important and as the conversation progresses,

> 'Everyone sees and internally represents things slightly differently. The better I understand those things, the more easily I can choose what to say and how to say it...'

any one of those ideas may turn out to be worth talking about, but for now let's not give the other person a drink with a fire-hose.

'Your purpose at this stage is not to persuade, but to set a platform to enable the other person to talk to you.

'Now, if they ask you to give an outline of your charity or your appeal, and you give it and then just stop, then the conversation will have ground to a halt.

'So, you have to have a clear intention that you'll throw the conversational ball back to them. How do you do that?'

'Well, I suppose you ask them questions.'

'Spot on. What sort of questions? Well, this isn't hard. You already do it. In my case, a fundamental thing is to find out if people have a pet themselves, and if it's a cat, a dog or something else. People who work for medical charities often find out whether the potential supporter knows someone who has suffered from that disease. Can you see how the answers to these questions and any subsequent chat it leads to will tell us some useful information about their world?'

'Sure, that makes sense. And one I often use is 'what caused them to start supporting us, or come to our event for the first time."

'Excellent, Claire. So the key thing is that you already know some sensible questions to ask. All I'm saying is, make sure you ask them nice and early in a conversation, before you say too much about your charity.

'Then there's one more idea to bear in mind, which is that you may sometimes need to make it more likely that they'll want to open up and answer those questions. After giving my summary, I usually just tell my potential donor that my summary is so brief because if I went into any more detail for now, it would be hard to make it relevant to them. So I can only make it interesting if I know a bit about them … and then I ask whatever question feels most appropriate.'

Freya's mobile rang, and while she answered it, Claire tidied up the notes she had been making. She wrote the following:

The heart of an influencing conversation:

After the initial warm up chit-chat at the start of a conversation, if you are asked to introduce your charity or proposal, initially <u>be very brief</u> ...

... so that you can ask them questions and properly <u>understand and appreciate</u> their world ...

... so that when you do describe your charity or proposal in more depth, you can <u>tailor what you say</u> and how you say it to suit their interests and communication style.

When Freya had finished her call, Claire said 'Well, this makes a lot of sense and I think there are times when I've done it naturally. It's just that some other times, with more difficult or powerful people, under the stress of the situation I've not done everything I can to make it easier for the other person to share their point of view early on.

'But tell me, it's not always going to work, is it? I mean, some people, my dad for instance, are much happier talking freely about themselves than other people. But is this really going to work with more private people?'

'Well, no system is guaranteed. Certainly, some people will be more willing and able to answer your questions than others. For the more private ones, you may have to do more of the talking early on to try and get the conversation going. So you may need to pre-frame your questions with an example or story of what your own experience has been before you ask them. It's true that you may still have some conversations which don't quite click into the level of mutual sharing that you're aiming for. But as long as you have the mind-set of always at least *trying* to better understand the other person before getting bogged down in too much depth about your charity or new proposal, this has to be better than succumbing to the path of least resistance and doing most of the talking at the start.'

'That makes sense. Okay, so one last question. Where do I ask the person if they'd like to make a donation or explore a possible corporate partnership?'

'Again, there are exceptions to every rule … but my aim would be to ask them to take the next step on this journey of supporting your hospice after you have told them persuasive things about Alice House that match something you've found out they care about. The three steps you've jotted down are designed to maximise the chances that they'll say "You're doing great work in an area that is really important, how can I help?"

'And once you sense they have this feeling, whether or not they say it out loud, is where you tell them ways they could help.'

'And how do you know what to say, to cause them to feel that keen to help?' Claire asked.

Freya looked at Mark.

He answered, 'That I can help you with, but for now I suggest you've got enough to get your head around. If you can go and test out what changes when you apply the second law, I will help you with what to say after that in another meeting.'

Claire warmly thanked them for their time and Freya wished her luck. Then Claire hurried back to Bounds Green tube.

Back at Alice House, Claire spent the whole afternoon at her desk, preparing for the four meetings with potential supporters that she had scheduled for later that week. She found the ideas that Freya had explained were very helpful. Although she could not be certain what these people would talk about, it was reassuring to start planning how she might encourage them to open up.

• THE SECOND LAW •
THE LAW OF
UNDERSTANDING

—

IF YOU WANT TO
INFLUENCE SOMEONE,
FIRST UNDERSTAND
AND APPRECIATE
THEIR WORLD

—

CHAPTER 4

The **THIRD** law

Two weeks after they'd met at The North London Dogs Home, Claire received an email from Mark inviting her to meet him in The Breakfast Club, a trendy coffee shop in Shoreditch.

When she arrived she saw Mark at a table in the far corner, listening to a man with his back to the room. Mark saw her and waved.

'Claire, this is my good friend, James. James, I'm really pleased to introduce you to Claire Hardie'.

Claire guessed James was in his early thirties. She warmed to him immediately.

'Mark told me you enjoyed your chat with Freya. I imagine she was helpful.' James said.

'Yes, she really was. And just in the last week her ideas have already helped. I've been working hard at finding ways to make it easier for the other person to talk more freely in a conversation. Freya's tips have prevented me from getting stranded by saying too much early on. Apart from anything else, being a bit more willing to direct the conversation, you can help the other person want to talk about themselves a lot more.'

'Yes, even just greater awareness of what you want to happen can be strangely effective, can't it, especially if that objective is a greater feeling in the other person that you want to understand.' He sipped his coffee. 'And I'm assuming Mark set up this chat because he thought we could help each other. Is there something I could do for you?'

Claire looked at Mark, who proceeded to outline James' career over the past nine years. He had worked in three different fundraising teams, all at Stand Up for Children, and now he was head of new business in their corporate partnerships team.

'That's right,' James added. 'It's my job to build relationships with the companies that would make the biggest difference to the children that our charity helps.'

Putting down his cup, Mark explained why he'd wanted Claire to meet James.

·

'In James' first year in this role at Stand Up For Children, he has created six new important partnerships. That's apart from the new £5 million pound strategic partnership which he's just been telling me about.' Mark looked very proud of his friend.

'Claire, I've found that in fundraising, as in any industry, there are a lot of people who talk a good game. Maybe you heard a couple of them speak at the conference the other day ... and there are other people like James, who consistently get extraordinary results. I call these people bright spots. Throughout my career I've found you can learn an enormous amount if you seek them out. And although most people in the top 3% tend to have some moments of inspiration, I've found that the main reason they achieve results which are different and better than others is they have decided to adopt different habits. Day in, day out, James does some things slightly differently to the vast majority of corporate fundraisers. That's why his results are different.

> Day in, day out, James does some things slightly differently to the vast majority of corporate fundraisers. That's why his results are different.

'One of the things James is especially good at is influencing donors or companies when he meets them. The other day this knack helped him win a valuable partnership with a large high street bank.

'James, tell Claire why more companies and donors say "yes" to you than to other people.'

James looked at Claire. 'Well, I have had quite a few lucky breaks, but I agree with Mark that usually they come about because I focus on doing the basics of building trust and forming strong relationships with the right companies. This so-called *dream ten companies* strategy is easy to say and sometimes surprisingly hard to do. But before I carry on, it would be good to know a bit more about what you've been finding difficult when you talk to potential supporters.'

Claire told him how hard she had always found it to get donors to not only show interest, but to actually follow through and take action. When she could get people to come and visit Alice House they were often motivated by the place itself but if not, she rarely sensed she had helped them feel a connection to what the hospice stood for.

'So tell me James, apart from what Freya explained about the law of understanding, what do you think I should do?'

'Well my first principle, the rule that trumps all the rest, is I spend more time away from my desk, out talking to my existing and potential partners, than any normal fundraiser ever does. This is a lot easier said than done, which is why the few people who understand the idea in theory often struggle to achieve it in practice. But I'm not going to go into my techniques for succeeding at that, because Mark tells me you're already pretty good at getting people to meet you or attend your events.'

Claire felt pleased. She liked the idea that she was doing pretty well at what James considered to be the most important activity of all.

'But in terms of what makes me very confident, and often pretty successful at helping the donor or company want to support in some way ... I think the secret that Mark wanted me to show you is ... this'. James reached into his bag and pulled out a blue, hard-back A4 notebook. It was slightly faded. White cardboard was visible at a couple of the corners where the blue outer layer had worn away. 'It's all right here,' he said.

> 'Well my first principle, the rule that trumps all the rest, is I spend more time away from my desk, out talking to my existing and potential partners, than any normal fundraiser ever does.

'why do you say stories are so important? I see they could be useful for a certain sort of donor, but I'd never have called them *rocket fuel*.'

On the front of the book were the handwritten words *James' story bank – fundraising rocket fuel*.

'This,' he said with a smile, 'is my competitive edge,' and handed the notebook to Claire.

Intrigued, Claire opened the notebook and flicked through the pages. Inside, she found page after page of stories and anecdotes, mostly handwritten. Just occasionally there was a glued-in photocopy from a newspaper, or printed out document. Each entry was less than a page. Most of them consisted of a handwritten title, underlined, with four or five bullet-pointed sentences underneath.

The dates early in the book were four years ago. Claire didn't feel she had time to focus on any particular example but leafing through the book, the main impression she got was of discipline. It was fair to say that James did not have the neatest handwriting but she had a sense the collection had been assembled with great care.

'This is amazing. How did you collect so many?'

'Hmmm. I decided to, I guess,' James said.

'You decided …' For a moment, the thought occurred to Claire that perhaps all of Mark's laws were basically about making firm decisions that other people don't get round to making. She was beginning to understand what a powerful impact a clear decision makes on subsequent results. But surely there's more to it than that, she thought. And anyway, she didn't wholly understand why a collection of examples like she was looking at could be described as the source of a fundraiser's competitive advantage.

'It's an impressive collection, but surely case studies are only one element of what influences people. And they don't influence everybody do they?'

'You're right, case studies don't influence everyone. But these aren't case studies, at least not in the normal sense that that phrase is used in charities.'

'What's the difference?'

'Well, one of the things that is useful to include in a proposal is a case study. Usually, this is to do with what happened to one of the people who benefited from your charity's work. It's one element that's useful. But the problem is that normally, to send something you've written to ten or 10,000 people, the case study goes through a sign-off procedure within your charity. Though this is necessary, it is very rare that what started as a real example of what happened keeps that realness. So I use this book to collect spoken stories to help me whenever I talk to donors. That's why to me it's a collection of stories for telling verbally, as opposed to case studies which would be used in written form.'

'That makes sense, but there are several things I don't follow. Quite apart from the fact that in my charity it's really hard to get either case studies or stories … why do you say stories are so important? I see they could be useful for a certain sort of donor, but I'd never have called them *rocket fuel*.'

This made James laugh. 'Excellent question. The reality is that most people who work in fundraising have some sense that stories about what difference the charity makes could be interesting to some donors. A few even understand that it's also quite helpful to have examples that bring to life the problems experienced by their beneficiaries, that don't even mention your charity. But very few fundraisers have grasped that stories are *essential* if we are to become truly persuasive and confident when we meet donors. The third law is the law of firepower. It states that the fundraiser who collects, practises and knows more stories will find it easier to influence when in conversation with potential supporters.'

The third law – the law of firepower
'The fundraiser who collects, practises and knows more stories will find it easier to influence when in conversation with potential supporters.'

Mark allowed Claire to write this down and then added, 'What it really means is, to reach the higher levels of persuasiveness, you need to have gathered assets, some things in your pocket which you can deploy to convey any of the important ideas that might help someone want to give. When I started noticing the power of this law, I originally called it the law of resources. But the more I thought about it, the more I decided that talking about resources sounds dry. No metaphor is perfect, but I changed it to the law of firepower because it gives me a sense of the energy that having great stories brings to your ability to influence.'

James continued, 'Have you ever seen a programme called Dragon's Den?'

'Sure.'

'Well, on Dragon's Den, I think the first problem the would-be entrepreneurs have is to show whether their product is any good. Actually, there are other things they also have to successfully persuade on, but usually the first problem is whether or not their product even works. Well, I've noticed that there is nothing stronger in convincing the investors than some kind of demonstration. To me, that demo is just one kind of story which helps the audience see that the product works. Now, lots of stories aren't physical demonstrations but they have many things in common with them.

'So my question to you is, if you agree that "stories" or tangible human examples are useful to someone trying to persuade someone else, what is it about stories that helps? How do stories help the person who is seeking to influence the other?'

Claire's brow furrowed as she tried to understand what he was getting at. But, as soon as she understood what James was asking, two or three answers occurred to her.

She told him that stories were one way of showing evidence of impact for her hospice's patients; they were also a means of conveying complex ideas, in a simple, accessible way, the way journalists often do; they were more memorable than other ways of talking, and more likely to hold people's attention than other things you might say about a charity, like its mission statement or strategy.

James added that stories tend to evoke feelings. And not just the intense, negative emotions like sadness or shock that many people associate with some famous charity campaigns, but the full range, like pride and excitement and hope. 'In fact,' concluded James, 'we could very easily go on and list a dozen reasons why stories, examples and anecdotes are the friend of anyone in the influencing business.'

'Okay, so I get that they're very useful. But your job now is in corporate fundraising. I thought the main reason that a company partners with a charity is to help increase profit, either by warming

> 'In fact,' concluded James, 'we could very easily go on and list a dozen reasons why stories, examples and anecdotes are the friend of anyone in the influencing business.'

up their brand, improving employee morale or helping sell more washing powder or whatever.'

'I agree; some kind of commercial benefit is usually the primary driver for most corporate partnerships with charities.'

'So, why are stories about how you help the people who benefit from your charity's services so important to a company?'

'There are two answers. Firstly, every company is made up of people, and people are influenced by stories, assuming your cause is something that those employees could feel strongly about. It is rare that a company considers a partnership with a charity that does not strike a chord with some of its employees or customers.

'Secondly, it's true that I do use stories about our cause when I meet or pitch to someone from a company. But we need to be clear that these are not the only type of story, or necessarily the most important. I agree with what you said that the primary driver for the company is usually that this partnership with a charity will help the company in some way. Now obviously, for it to genuinely be a partnership, both partners need to benefit, and for the charity a key part of this is usually funding. So in terms of other kinds of story, have you heard of *social proof*?'

'No, I don't think so.'

'There's a fascinating book by Robert Cialdini called *Influence, Science and Practice*,' James explained. 'He describes the six weapons of influence used by skilful influencers of all professions. Weapon number three on this list, Cialdini calls social proof.'

He paused, then asked 'Why do you think some companies deliberately tell us how popular they are with straplines like "nine out of ten cats prefer it" or "the world's favourite airline"?'

Claire didn't need to think hard about this. She replied 'Well, it makes them seem popular and they must think you're then more likely to buy. But surely intelligent people don't fall for that? If you've got half a brain you weigh up how good you think the cat food or the airline is for yourself ...'

'You'd think so, wouldn't you? And I used to think the same. One thing that helped me wise up was the busking experiment. Do you think that if an accomplice of a busker walks past her hat and places coins in it at regular intervals, the number of coins that other passers-by give would increase?'

Claire thought for a moment. 'Yes, I suppose it would.'

'By how much?'

'I don't know, twenty percent … maybe thirty percent more money in the hat?'

'That's what I'd have guessed. In fact, the income goes up by *eight times*. So for example, rather than making £10 in a busking session, their income would increase not to £12 or £13 as you just guessed, but to £80. You'd make £80 instead of £10. That, Claire, is the power of social proof.

'The more you read about Cialdini's six weapons of influence, the less naïve you become about the real factors that affect people's buying (or in our case, giving) decisions.

'The reality is that there is a limit to the processing power of the human brain. So it takes shortcuts. And one of these shortcuts is to look at what people similar to ourselves are doing, to help us make our decision. This social proof effect is so powerful precisely because we're often unaware of the real reasons we make decisions. Apparently, when interviewed by researchers, none of the people who put money in the busker's hat said they had done so because they saw someone else do it. They all said other things, such as they liked the music or were feeling generous.

'So a vital tool for any corporate fundraiser is stories about other companies who have partnered with your charity and got benefit from doing so. I imagine you've already got some partnerships with companies, haven't you?'

'Sure, corporate partnerships is half my job.'

'And do you work hard on those events or cause related marketing projects that you do with them?'

'Yes, really hard. They always want everything as soon as possible.

And there's so much to do to make even the simplest event successful.'

'And do these partnerships usually work? Obviously, I hope they raise you as much money as the company agreed, but do these partnerships actually generate any business benefit to the company? Or was it all a ruse?'

'Well yes, of course they do. We organised a sponsored bike ride during the Tour de France using exercise machines for a French-owned insurance company a couple of months ago and my contact there was delighted. He said it brought out the competitiveness and the team spirit in everyone, because each division really wanted to win, and even all of the directors were getting involved. He said the office was still buzzing a week later.'

'That's excellent. So you made good on your promise from the start that partnering your charity would lift morale and teamwork in the company.'

'Absolutely,' said Claire with certainty.

'So, my question is, how many companies have you met since this event?'

'Err, two or three, I think.'

'And how many did you tell this story to?'

'I see your point. None. But then it didn't really come up and I don't even know how relevant it would have been.'

'I understand. And there are some companies that this particular social proof story would not be appropriate for. But unless you have systematically sought and practised the stories which demonstrate that partnering your charity does genuinely add value to its corporate partners, you won't be able to proactively drop them into conversation or pitch when appropriate. And while the company may nod at your claims that partnership with you will achieve business benefits, and they may even want to believe it's true, you will not have created what the pitch coach Oren Klaff calls a *wanting*. But if you give a real example, the other person will feel this wanting like a horse looking at a big juicy apple.

'The few corporate fundraisers who back up their claims with how much value they've added to other companies don't have to work nearly so hard to convince and persuade in the traditional sense, because what they say about the new potential partnership becomes easier to believe.

Claire sat back and drank some tea.

'This really is different from the way I've treated these conversations before. No wonder they're usually not that interested, even though they pretend to be. It's because at some subconscious level they thought I wanted them to treat the idea of a corporate partnership philanthropically, even though we dressed it up in the language of business benefit and partnership. But you're saying that if I learn to use these stories they'll start to genuinely feel this wanting for the partnership for their own reasons, in addition to any personal desire to do good.

'But one more thing is bothering me. Most of the companies I've dealt with seem to be most interested in facts and figures. That's certainly what they say to me.'

'Sure they do. And I suggest you keep doing whatever you're doing to find out the numbers, in terms of money raised, or how much it costs to fund a bed at Alice House for a year, or whatever. Know the numbers of course. But don't believe the lie that saying numbers in their purest state will persuade anyone to do anything.'

'But that's what everyone does. Are you telling me they're wrong?'

'I'm saying that just because most fundraisers start explanations about their charity by telling us about their cleverly phrased strategy or big numbers about the prevalence of a particular medical condition ... just because this is the

'...just because this is the normal way that charities talk, does not make it the smartest way we could help our audience understand and care.'

normal way that charities talk, does not make it the smartest way we could help our audience understand and care.

'We have to be smarter than that and make our own decision as to what would be the most effective way of stimulating our audience's willingness help.'

'And what about with major donors or associations like the Rotary Clubs that might want to partner with us? Do Cialdini's techniques like social proof work in these other types of fundraising?'

'Absolutely. If you phone the chair of a Rotary Club to persuade him to meet you, be able to succinctly mention a specific way that a Lions Club's members got benefit when they last supported you.

James looked at his watch and looked apologetic. 'Forgive me, Claire, I'm going to have to get away to my next meeting now. And you look a little shell-shocked. But I hope some of these ideas have been useful. If so, what are the main things you've taken from our conversation?'

Claire paused as she tried to get to grips with what she thought about it all.

'Yes, firstly, it's been ever so helpful, and thanks so much for making time to show me some of your techniques.

'Secondly, I think the main thing is that although I've always done my best to prepare before meeting my potential supporters, I wasn't preparing this sort of thing. And I think the reason why is because if someone talked about stories in fundraising before, I had far too narrow a definition of what that meant. I feel like my whole way of thinking about, well, not just stories, but preparing for what to say to supporters in general ... I see this whole topic differently now.'

Mark looked happy. 'Thanks James, your work is done. Best of luck in your next meeting.'

James got up to go. 'Oh, I nearly forgot, I brought you a present.' He held out a red paperback book to Claire. The cover read: *The Small BIG*, Robert Cialdini, Steve Martin and Noah Goldstein.

• THE THIRD LAW •
THE LAW OF
FIREPOWER

—

THE FUNDRAISER
WHO COLLECTS,
PRACTISES AND KNOWS
MORE STORIES WILL
FIND IT EASIER TO
INFLUENCE WHEN
IN CONVERSATION
WITH POTENTIAL
SUPPORTERS

—

CHAPTER 5

The story success habit

Claire felt exhilarated with the conversation so far, and was touched that James had thought to bring her the book, and yet suddenly she felt weary.

'Are you alright?' asked Mark.

'Yeah, I'm fine. But I feel the two of you have opened my eyes to the sorts of material I should be gathering and practising to be able to tell people about our hospice ... but my main realisation is that I just don't have anywhere near enough stories of any kind. I mean, I get that they're not going to be handed to me on a plate, but it feels so daunting to go from the two or three sketchy half-anecdotes that I have now, to the kind of bank of content that James has. I don't know where to start.'

'That makes sense. Let's get out of here and get moving. It'll help clear our heads and find the energy to make sense of this different perspective.' They turned left out of the café and started to walk.

Mark continued 'When my way of understanding something gets jolted like this, I tend to get a sort of exhilaration closely followed by the realisation that there are still more questions than answers. Now if that's how you feel, I have two ideas that might help.

'Firstly, a mentor once advised me not to fight the feeling of confusion, because counter-intuitive though this sounds, some kind of breakthrough is usually on its way to you. You are most likely to notice this breakthrough insight if you accept the confusion and be curious about it. Don't worry that everything is not yet solved. Practise having faith that you're on the way to solving it.'

'Hmm. Well okay, I'll do my best. What's the other thing?'

'The other thing? Oh yes. Well, it seems to me that a lot of what's daunting now is that you've realised you don't have much persuasive content. Seeing James' story notebook has been helpful but it also gives you a sense of the mountain ahead of you. If you stay overwhelmed by the mountain you might not even start climbing.'

'Yes, that's it. I do feel overwhelmed.'

'Well for that one, an idea that helped me is an ancient Chinese saying: the best time to plant a woodland is thirty years ago. The second best time is now.'

Claire thought that one over. 'I suppose you're right. It's far better to have your awareness heightened of what the gap is that you need to fill, than to have not been aware of it at all. But do you have any tips that will make it easier to start collecting stories in the first place?'

'...the best time to plant a woodland is thirty years ago. The second best time is now.'

'Yes, I have ideas that will enable you to know and confidently tell dozens of persuasive, tangible stories. If you asked me whether it's easy, I'd have to say no, it's not easy, otherwise people who are not committed could do it as well as James or you. That's why success will always elude people who think the law of decision is not for them. Is it entirely do-able without a great deal of arduous labour? Absolutely. I've seen dozens and dozens of fundraisers raise more money by gradually building up the number of stories and specific examples they have at their fingertips.'

The brisk walk and fresh air was working wonders and Claire felt her sense of optimism returning.

'So come on then, Mark. What do I have to do to create a collection of lucrative stories like James has?'

'Well, what I shared with James four years ago, and have shown to various committed fundraisers since, is a three step formula. Now, while a few fundraisers, without knowing the formula as such, do one or two of these steps to some degree, I've found that fewer than 1 in a 100 consistently apply all three steps.

'But James only managed to include so many persuasive stories in his million pound pitch to the high street bank the other day because he's been applying all three steps for the last few years.'

'So, what's the formula?'

'Choose; lock in; use'.

The story success habit: choose; lock in; use.

Mark looked at her. Then he carried on: 'Step one. Choose. You have to decide, am I going to focus on story? Will I treat anecdote and concrete human example as the most valuable tool at my disposal? Or, will I not? Will I treat it as the ultimate rocket fuel to power me to extraordinary fundraising success?

'If you treat stories with curiosity and hunger you will start to notice them everywhere. You will talk differently to your colleagues. You won't send them an email asking them for "evidence of impact". You'll call them up or just chat face to face and ideally persuade them to meet you. When you do meet, or hear them give a presentation, you'll combine the strengths of a determined detective with those of a curious, charming journalist. Whenever you talk to colleagues who work with patients or their families, you'll listen out for stories, and if you don't hear any you'll specifically ask questions to find the key elements that make up a story. The whole game starts with a decision to *value* story.

'Step two. Lock in. One of the reasons story is so powerful is that it sticks in people's memories. There's a fascinating book about this called *Made to Stick* by Chip and Dan Heath. But although they are more memorable than most other things you could say, even if people do value story, most over-estimate their own ability to remember and make use of the stories they hear. There's a difference between remembering the gist of it two months later and knowing it with the confidence that you'd need to proactively introduce it into an important conversation with a donor.'

'When you do meet, or hear them give a presentation, you'll combine the strengths of a determined detective with those of a curious, charming journalist.'

'Really? Surely everyone understands that you have to work at this sort of thing?'

'In the abstract, maybe. But in practice, when it's a bit inconvenient, we lie to ourselves.'

They found themselves at a small, threadbare patch of grass and sat down on a bench. Claire was looking sceptical, so Mark added 'I was once training fundraisers at one of the most famous charities in the world. At lunch time they invited me to join them to listen to a talk given by one of their programme staff just back from distributing emergency supplies in Pakistan, where there had been an earthquake. I was in a conference room with about forty-five other people, mostly fundraisers, from the famous charity. A lot of what the programme worker said was quietly inspiring. She told a couple of fantastic stories which brought to life what a difference donations were making to people's lives. I was delighted and wrote down both stories. While I was doing so, I looked around me to see who else was capturing this fundraising gold with as much satisfaction as I was. Here's my question, Claire. Guess how many people, out of the forty-five, were writing down the stories?'

'I don't know, maybe twenty?'

'Fat chance. In fact, only half a dozen even had a pen and paper with them. And only two other people in the room of forty-five were writing the stories down. Two out of forty-five! I know this because I was so amazed after the first story that I watched really carefully during the second one.' In the context of the conversation she'd just had in the café, Claire found this astonishing. But then she thought about it. She remembered that only last week, when

'only two other people in the room of forty-five were writing the stories down. *Two out of forty-five!*'

she had sat in on a talk from her head of care, although she had taken a pen and notepad with her, she had not written any stories down. The talk had been so interesting she'd decided to just listen. But now she realised that she could barely remember the specifics of anything the doctor had said.

'There are plenty of fundraisers who'd say stories are important, but they're convinced they work for an organisation that doesn't provide them with any, and that the lack of stories is either due to their type of cause (for instance charities which focus on research) or because it's someone else's fault.

'And because it's someone else's fault, they have no sense that they could find some juicy content themselves. So, in the understandable busy-ness of their fundraising deadlines, it becomes normal to not have or use many stories, while reserving the right to bemoan that someone in their charity should be providing them. I'm sure that if they wanted to, fundraisers at every charity in the country could find a way to believe that they were hard done by in this way. This sense of injustice is very seductive, but it robs them of their power to go and solve the problem.

'But here's my point of view, which is of course easier once you adopt a definition of story or tangible example that is much broader than *case study someone has documented about our services*. These same people who swear to me that they don't have access to enough stories still read news in the papers or on the internet, they still watch films, they read books, most of them occasionally hear talks from the chief executive or the researchers or academics, they may even have friends who have first-hand experience of their charity's issue ... and all the while they don't notice the gold slipping through their fingers.

'Once you've decided to really prioritise and value stories by creating a home to help lock them in, you will not only notice ones you would otherwise have ignored, but you will also be more organised in storing them. And once you start keeping them, your collection will grow from two to five to ten, very quickly. You don't need to compare yourself to James for a year or two yet, just compare yourself with the fundraiser you were last week. Who's going to be more confident walking to a meeting with a donor, the fundraiser who barely knows two stories, or the fundraiser who has sought out and captured ten?

'But they still won't raise you a single extra penny if you leave them languishing in your story file like you're some miserly collector of precious species. They only pay you back for this effort if you do step three, which is to *use* them!'

'So, step three means you tell them to donors?'

'Well, clearly that's the end goal but, in order to do that, a lot of what I mean is to dare to practise and share them so that they become a normal way to talk. Obviously, reading them through will help with this, but it's also so much easier to tell a story to a donor if you have previously heard yourself tell it competently to a colleague.

'And then yes, absolutely, you have to be prepared to use them when you talk to donors or companies. When you're nervous this can be harder to remember to do than it sounds, not least because I've never had a donor who said to me "what I'd really love to hear, Mark, is a story". Donors and companies ask you plenty of questions, like "do your services make a difference?" or "if we partnered with you, what would you want to tell our employees that would make them want to help?" ... to these questions, many of the best answers are stories. But to interpret the questions in this way, we have to have prepared in advance.

'One of the tactics I've found to improve my meeting technique is to use what I call **The Fundraiser's Meeting Checklist***, which contains the seven things I'm going to focus on when I meet a donor or company. To run through in my head the range of stories that are most likely to be helpful to that kind of supporter is point number five on my checklist.

'And of course, the more you use anything, the more you iron out the glitches.

* *To claim your free copy of The Fundraiser's Meeting Checklist, go to www.brightspotfundraising.co.uk/book-free-gift/*

'So, there you have it: Choose; lock in; use.

'Like most things I teach, each step is fairly obvious when you really think about it. And each step is also fairly simple, in that it's entirely do-able. I mean, even if we're often busy, which of us is unable to start a file, take and use a notebook when meeting our colleagues from the front line, make notes, store them and occasionally share them with colleagues, for example in team meetings? Anyone can do each of these steps in theory. But the question is, *will* you do these things week in, week out, even when you've got other things on your plate?

If you find the discipline to follow through on these three steps, you can shape your fundraising career path as you want it

'The answer to that question will determine how persuasive and confident you will become over the coming weeks, months and years. If you find the discipline to follow through on these three steps, you can shape your fundraising career path as you want it, including in terms of your level of responsibility, and the level of salary you're able to secure.'

Claire had been scribbling notes. Some of them weren't very legible, but she felt confident she'd captured the main ideas. Checking her watch, she thanked Mark for his help and set off for the tube.

CHAPTER 6

Rocket fuel

Claire opened her eyes in the darkness. She felt strangely alert, and yet as she looked at her alarm clock the fluorescent numbers distinctly read 6.02, and it wasn't even a week day. Her brain was working overtime, thoughts about fundraising and stories were appearing and colliding off each other at high speed. Some of them were practical ideas as she half-remembered anecdotes from the hospice and some of them were flights of fancy as she dreamed up what a fabulous fundraising career might look like.

'This is nuts. And on a Saturday,' she muttered, rolling over. 'Got to get back to sleep.' But the more she tried to switch off, the more insistently the thoughts surged through her.

By 6.30 she had decided to stop fighting it. She opened the curtains, crept quietly downstairs and made a cup of tea. Then she came back upstairs and got back into bed. Sitting up, looking out at the dawn light, she cradled the warmth of her tea and smiled. There was a time when a lie-in at the weekend was as important a goal as anything in her life. And now, as she enjoyed feeling excited, she realised that waking up with this sense of purpose was another sign that she had begun to believe. Yes, that was it. At some deep level she was now able to believe that really great progress was possible, even for her. And this realisation changed everything.

Claire sat up in bed for the next half hour, allowing the thoughts that had woken her up to ebb and flow. In her early teens she had sometimes had difficulty sleeping and her mum had taught her to keep a notepad and pen by the side of the bed. She had found that when she gave in to her racing mind and captured her thoughts on paper, she could usually switch off and get back to sleep.

So sometime after seven, she went and grabbed her notebook and a pen from her bag, and again came back to bed and enjoyed capturing the dominant ideas that had woken her up.

The cause for her excitement, she decided, was that much of James' success derived from his being more hungry for stories, and more thorough in how he filed and practised them, than anyone she had met. This was fundamentally different to what her view had always been of successful, persuasive, confident people. And the more this point of view took hold, the more she could not help but look directly at its implications. Picking up her pen, she captured the thought on paper.

If he can do it, why shouldn't I?
And, if he can do it, so can I!

Whereas most of her notes were in her usual, neat handwriting, she had found herself emblazoning these letters in large capitals, filling a half a page.

Some of her notes had been an attempt to capture her stream of consciousness. More or less, this was an action list of things she wanted to do.

A thought had been nagging at her and again she found herself giving in to these irrational, distinctly un-Claire-like impulses. She put on her dressing gown and rummaged around in the box under her desk.

She found an old ring binder file. Switching on her laptop and printer, she printed *Fundraising stories* on a white label.

The cause for her excitement, she decided, was that much of James' success derived from his being more hungry for stories, and more thorough in how he filed and practised them, than anyone she had met.

Then she stopped. At some point she remembered Mark had told her that the precise words we choose matter. This is true when we're talking to donors and colleagues but even more than this, to ourselves.

The key point she had taken from meeting James was not sophisticated but she sensed it would make all the difference. The fundamental difference between James and most fundraisers she had met was that he *valued* stories. She believed that it would pain James to ever hear a specific example or story and fail to take five minutes to write it up and file it.

'How has he conditioned himself to be so uncompromising?' she wondered.

Mark had also told her that like her, there had been a period in James' career when he'd felt nothing was working. In hitting rock bottom he had found a new resolve to do things differently. And that probably accounted for his intense drive to follow through. But there was something else James seemed to do. Claire reached again for her notes and remembered what James had written on the front of his notebook. '*Story bank – fundraising rocket fuel.*' When she'd read it Claire had found this weird. We're in England, not California, for goodness sake. But then it wasn't intended to help anyone else, was it? It clearly worked for him. She realised that that was where some of James's edge came from. When other fundraisers heard a concrete human example, they thought of it as 'a case study', and failed to follow up accordingly. When James heard the same thing he was seeing it as rocket fuel for fundraising success. She knew which she'd find easier to find time to write down and remember. No wonder he had built up a file of more than sixty stories, whereas most people knew only one or two which they could barely remember.

Claire went to the red file and peeled off the label she had printed. She folded it in half, then ripped it neatly in two and dropped it in the waste paper basket. Then, smiling, she typed out a new label. She stuck it to her folder and held the

> No wonder he had built up a file of more than sixty stories, whereas most people knew only one or two which they could barely remember.

folder up at arm's length, admiring her handiwork. She read back to herself '*Story gold to persuade and inspire*'. She found that during the five minutes it had taken her to change the label, she had started to feel even more optimistic.

She divided the file into two: **Stories about the cause and our services** and **Social proof stories** — *companies and donors who have gained emotionally or practically by supporting.*

She racked her brains and was pleased to jot down a couple of good anecdotes that she'd heard her chief executive repeat in two or three presentations to supporters. Then she thought back to her first and only meeting with the head of the care team at Alice House and could remember the gist of something she'd said. But she couldn't remember enough detail to tell it with any conviction to a supporter. She found this depressing. But then it struck her. She would have to go to the source.

For weeks now she'd been meaning to go and sit in on the care team's weekly meeting, but never quite got round to following through because she'd always been stressed about how much work she had to do. Mark had mentioned that even three years into his job, James made it his business to find chances to talk to the social workers who worked with children as often as he possibly could. Apparently, he was regularly tempted to cancel these visits, but his discipline in repeatedly investing effort in these conversations with the people on the front line gave him a competitive advantage whenever he was in front of a potential supporter.

> James' discipline in repeatedly investing effort in these conversations with the people on the front line gave him a competitive advantage...

Mark said that James' edge came in three forms – his drive – every time he returned from hearing about the children his efforts would help, he found he needed less willpower to get himself to take action. Secondly, it was where he got most of his stories. And thirdly, the knowledge it gave him of how donors' money was spent increased the aura of confidence and credibility he projected to donors, whether or not he told them any stories.

Claire put the file away and wrote down in her journal what she had decided to do on Monday morning. There were plenty of other things to sort out on Monday, but by lunch time she was determined to see if she could get permission to sit in on the weekly meeting of the care team.

Then she put away her story folder and her journal and went downstairs to find some breakfast.

CHAPTER 7
The **FOURTH** law

T he lift doors glided open without a sound. Mark and Claire stepped out onto the plush, royal blue carpet in the lobby of the 19th floor. Everything about this office was designed to suggest wealth and power.

They signed in and waited for Mark's contact to arrive from within the bank.

Five minutes later, an attractive Asian woman in her forties walked briskly into the lobby.

'Claire, this is Nila,' said Mark.

Mark briefly explained to Nila that he was helping Claire with her research into fundraising influence. He told her how in just two weeks Claire had found time to gather more than a dozen stories, examples and bits of social proof that might help a donor value the services her hospice provided.

'That's fantastic, Claire. Have you had time to do any of your other work?'

Claire laughed. 'Just about. Actually, I found the most efficient way to get amazing content was to sit in on the care team's weekly meeting. I don't know why I never did it before. It was the most fascinating and inspiring part of my week by a mile. And the extra effort is already paying off. To be honest, in most of my phone calls and the couple of donor meetings I've had, I haven't specifically known how or when to use the stories themselves, but in spite of this, I think just knowing in more depth what our charity is all about has made me more confident.'

Mark seemed pleased. 'That's really excellent; good for you. Apart from anything else, you're probably feeling more confident because you've got your mojo back. And that's a happy by-product of taking action towards a goal of your choosing, rather than feeling powerless to change your circumstances.'

Claire thought about this and agreed she had definitely felt bolder and more energised since she had become proactive about developing her skills.

Mark turned to Nila. 'So, thanks for making time for us, Nila. More than most people you'll ever meet, Claire now values stories and is developing the habit of seeking them out. Today I wanted you to help her understand how and when to use them. Perhaps we could start by explaining what you do for Jardines.'

'Sure. Well Claire, my background is in fundraising; I started out working for a small charity that funds research into bowel cancer. But, in a sense, I'm now on the other side of the fence.' She took a thick, cream-coloured business card from a leather case and passed it to Claire. 'I'm now the philanthropy advisor here at Jardines Bank. It's my job to help our clients, most of whom are very wealthy, to achieve their philanthropic goals.'

'What a fascinating job.'

'It most certainly is.'

'Every month,' Mark added, 'Nila works with clients who are donating sums of five, six or seven figures. How many wealthy people do you think you've worked with, Nila?'

'I'm really not sure, I've not counted. But I've been here for fourteen years, so I guess I must have helped between 650 and 700 clients with their philanthropy.

'And in that time I've also seen a huge number of fundraising proposals … and I've met a fair few fundraisers from all sorts of charities.'

Now Claire understood why she was here. Nila must have seen how millions, perhaps billions of pounds had been given away.

'As such, Nila is pretty well placed to understand which pitches and proposals tend to succeed and which ones fail.'

'What an insight you must have. Tell me, are there some factors that are common to the proposals that succeed, or does it vary as greatly as

> ... she had definitely felt bolder and more energised since she had become proactive about developing her skills.

the interests of your clients?'

'Good question. But before I answer it, I haven't properly understood your background, and I've found I can best bring these ideas to life when I know your situation. So how long have you worked for Alice House?'

Claire explained a bit of her background and as she did so, she realised it would have been so easy for Nila to talk at her without first finding out about her. Most people would have steamed ahead. She realised that one reason she had connected so readily with James' ideas was that he too had not rushed in to his explanation, but had first applied the law of understanding, and carefully found out about her so that he could understand and appreciate her world.

After a few minutes getting to know Claire, Nila started to explain what she had learned when she started at the bank. 'For the first few weeks in my job, I thought it was pretty random, but then the pattern emerged, and once I saw it, it was clear as day.'

'So is there a system that wealthy people use for evaluating charity presentations?'

'No, most of my clients are not especially systematic. They may be wealthy, but they're as human as anyone else who cares about making the world a better place. People are people, with the same emotional needs and foibles, whether or not they own a Lear jet.'

'So, if there is a pattern to what causes people to choose to give, what is it?'

'Excellent question, which I will answer. But first, I've got a question for you. What do you think most fundraisers talk about first, if they are invited to pitch to one of our clients?'

'Well, probably they first talk about what the problem is for the people or animals they help, and then they explain how their charities solve it.'

'Good guess but you're wrong. Actually, what nearly all of them do is to talk about themselves, their own charity, at great length first, including their strategy and the services they provide.

'Though most of my clients are too polite to show it, at worst, this bores them senseless. And at best, it is certainly a missed opportunity.'

'So what should they do?'

'They should apply the fourth law of persuasive fundraising conversations – the law of contrast.

'This law states "The most certain way to help someone want to give is to evoke a problem they care about and then help them believe your charity is able to solve it".'

Claire wrote it down.

The fourth law – the law of contrast
'The most certain way to help someone want to give is to evoke a problem they care about and then help them believe your charity is able to solve it.'

'Now, I need to clarify this. It is sometimes true that fundraisers do touch on the problem – but the most typical way is to quote huge, brain-boggling statistics about the number of people afflicted by that disease or kind of violence or whatever. How do you react if I tell you that each year one million children die of starvation in sub-Saharan Africa? Or, so many hundred women die of breast cancer per year? Be as honest as you can, what does it cause you to feel?'

'Well, maybe I should feel something, and I suppose I'm intellectually quite concerned, but in terms of feelings, I don't even know how I feel. If anything, the numbers are so huge that I feel it's all a bit hopeless. What difference can I make?'

'That's right', Nila replied. 'Mother Theresa once said, 'if I look at the mass I never act. If I look at the one, I will."

'Okay', said Claire, 'so you're saying I shouldn't tell my supporters that, for example, 300,000 people are diagnosed with life-limiting illnesses every year.'

'No Claire, I'm saying that could be a valuable fact, but only when the key barrier to the supporter continuing their conversation with you is the need for this sense of how numerically large this situation is. Some trusts or companies may need to know this at some point. But in most conversations you'll have, the sheer scale of the problem is rarely the most interesting or persuasive idea.'

Nila took another sip of her tea before continuing, 'Right now, unless we catch their interest and help them feel, rather than think, that hospice care matters to them, we've let them down.'

This made sense to Claire. She asked, 'Okay, so how do you do that?'

'Well, let me ask you a question, Claire. I understand that there are not enough hospice beds in any part of the UK to meet demand. So do you know what is difficult for patients diagnosed with advanced stages of motor neurone disease or Parkinson's disease or cancer, that don't have the option of coming to Alice House?' Nila seemed genuinely curious.

'If they don't have access to a place at the hospice?' Claire thought for a moment. 'Oh well, all sorts of things are hard. I don't know what your experience of most hospitals is like, but whenever I've been there, the staff are working really hard, but they've just been too stretched. So that means sometimes you could be waiting for up to four hours for someone to check in on you, so you might be in pain for longer than you needed to be. And there's also something that seems more abstract, but which is actually really important, which is being treated like an individual, rather than a number to be processed ...

'So, the time I was in hospital having my appendix out, at least I had my parents coming in to keep me company. But if you're in your sixties or seventies, you've maybe got no family and you've got cancer at an advanced stage, just how much more important would it be that you can get pain relief and company whenever you need it? You see, at Alice House there is so much more focus on the patient, because each nurse only looks after two patients ...'

'Excellent, Claire.' Nila was holding up her hand. 'So, you just described to me two of the problems which I imagine Dame Cicely Saunders was aiming to solve when she pioneered the early versions of hospice care at St Christopher's Hospice in the nineteen fifties and sixties. Namely, in a busy public hospital, patients with serious illnesses can sometimes not receive enough one to one care from nurses, which means that they can sometimes wait for too long without, for example, receiving adequate pain relief or something else that would make them feel comfortable. And the second problem you pointed out was that when you are looked after in a hospital, the medical staff are so busy that what gets focused on above all are the medical issues. And other things, like the patients' emotional, psychological and spiritual needs – which, when you think about it, all have a huge impact on well-being – can be neglected.'

'Yes, I didn't put it quite that way but, however hard the staff in a hospital work – and the ones I've met do truly care and work incredibly hard – both the things you said can be a real problem. Whereas at Alice House ...'

Again, Nila held up her hand, smiling. 'Hang on! You see how tempting it is to tell me about how wonderful Alice House is? Just now you were doing so well at the first part of the law of contrast, which is to help me tune in to how bad the problem is, but then you couldn't help but tell me something great about Alice House, which was the fantastically low ratio of nurses to patients. This is one of your best cards so don't use it too early. Do you remember what question I asked you?'

'You said "What is so difficult for patients who have life-limiting illnesses like advanced stage cancer?"'

'Right, so for now, let's just focus on that. The law of contrast asserts that we'll be most persuasive if we only do the second part, that is, showing that our solution works, after we have done the first part, that is, help them feel the problem, properly.'

'Well, that makes sense in theory, but I'm now realising it's harder to do in practice than it looks.'

'Absolutely. And this is progress, because that realisation is half the battle.

'So now we're able to be really clear about one of the problems, that nurses are often over-stretched, and that this can have an impact on some patient's well-being. Maybe many people are starting to understand what we're talking about, at least intellectually. But are they feeling the truth of this?'

'I'm not sure.'

'Ok, let's try another question. Do you know of anyone who's been in this situation?'

'Where not all of their needs have been met in hospital? I guess the example I find most difficult is what happened to the father of one of my friends. He was very poorly near the end, and he was in hospital, but my friend used to be furious when she found out that sometimes he wasn't eating because no one was helping him to eat. She'd get there and find that his food had just been left on a tray in front of him and he hadn't touched it. She couldn't understand why no one was taking responsibility for whether he was eating anything.'

'So he wasn't eating at all'?'

'Well sometimes he was, but she said that other day's his breakfast hadn't been touched. She did her best to tell the nurses so sometimes it got better. But she got so stressed when she had to leave each afternoon, wondering whether anyone would help him eat or drink in the evening and at breakfast till she got there the next day.'

'That's so difficult.'

'Yes it was. She was really upset.'

'And now do you think you've helped me tune in to what one of the problems in a busy hospital can be?' Nila asked.

'Yes, I think so. I think you connected to the problem.'

'And how did you do it?'

'Well, I gave you a specific example.'

'That's it,' said Nila. 'Just like any decent journalist preparing a news story would have done, you brought the general idea to life through the specific. Now the reason you may not have ordinarily talked about your friend's Dad to supporters before is that examples like this are not even about your hospice. Your colleagues are unlikely to have ever recorded anecdotes like this. Because they're an example of the opposite of hospice care.

'There's one more question that I often find useful in working out the first part of the law of contrast.' Nila continued, 'What is not obvious about the problem, or why it occurs? For instance, do you think the nurses on your friend's father's ward were deliberately callous?'

'Well I don't know. I do think that someone should have taken responsibility, but no, I don't think he was deliberately ignored.' Claire thought about it. 'There probably just wasn't a system for whose responsibility it was, and they each thought someone else had done it. Or maybe, when they're incredibly busy, it increases the likelihood that whatever system you have, it will fail at some point. I heard that, in most public hospitals, there is on average one nurse assigned to look after at least nine patients.'

'Excellent point. I'm sure many hospitals solve this problem in spite of this difficult ratio, but equally I imagine it's not easy.'

'But I don't want to make the supporter I'm talking to miserable do I? I hate those adverts that just shock you with how awful things are.'

'A fair point, and I wouldn't recommend that you ever focus the donor's attention on a difficult story like this and then walk out the door. But remember that this is just the first part of the fourth law. But without background, it is almost impossible to appreciate foreground.'

'But without background, it is almost impossible to appreciate foreground.'

'So I think I follow some of the ways to help the supporter emotionally understand the problem. How do you suggest I do the second part?'

'Well what most people do now is talk about what their charity does to make that problem better. But, sensible though this sounds, it's not the best thing to focus on.'

Claire was confused. 'So you're saying to evoke the problem and then show the donor how you solve it ... is wrong.'

'Well I wouldn't say it's "wrong" ... but it's not the most effective way to help someone decide to take action to make things better.'

'So what should you do instead?'

'Above all, help me feel that your charity's solution makes a difference. If the mother of fundraising influence is help me tune into the problem, then the father is help me feel and believe your solution works.'

Claire knew perfectly well that you need to find ways to convey impact to donors. But now that she thought about it, she realised it was true, she *did* usually spend far more time talking about how the hospice worked, what was great about it, than time showing that it was *effective*. In fact, she wondered if she had ever thought about them as two distinct concepts. But every fundraiser she knew tended to talk or write about the services that their charity provided. Maybe Nila was mistaken.

Nila saw Claire was processing what she'd said. She sipped her tea, and waited.

'It is true that I talk to our supporters about how the hospice works. But I always try and do it by presenting the benefits of any of the features I describe. And what's more, my supporters are often quite interested. They ask me about it.'

'I'm sure that some of them are interested,' said Nila, and then added, not unkindly, 'and how many of them then decide to make a donation?'

Claire winced inwardly. Whatever she had been doing up to now hadn't been very successful. Maybe the best test of any technique is the results it generates. 'Well, not many ... and I suppose that's your point. So you're saying I've got to show them that our hospice delivers on what we're there to do.'

'That's it.'

'Well, that makes sense in theory but, again, it's almost impossible in practice isn't it? I mean, my charity is just not set up to measure outcomes in the way that most companies would monitor their effectiveness.'

'Yes, I'm sure that's true. And a mistake that is easily made by people who originally worked in the corporate sector is that on discovering that monitoring of outcomes is inferior to what they would have expected, they conclude it is not possible to demonstrate impact. There are some charities that do manage to measure their effectiveness in a robust way but the reality is, many could do better.

'The first step to a better response to this issue is to try and understand why it might be. I think most charities are like this because they were not founded by people whose burning passion was to measure things. My sense is that the great movements for progress, the ones that have contributed most to alleviating suffering and improving the quality of millions of lives ... they all got started in the first place by people who felt inspired to go out and solve the problems that led to that suffering. The driving force that enabled them to keep going even when the odds were stacked against them, was not ... it was not the thrill of monitoring and measurement.

'So given that a focus on measurement may not already be a strong part of our culture, a good question to ask is "How could I work with my colleagues who deliver services to devise any means of measuring and demonstrating that our services make a difference?"

'Secondly, and more importantly, discovering our charity currently does not measure its effectiveness very well must not lead us to give up searching for answers to the question "How do we know that our service or our research makes things better for the people we serve?"'

Mark added, 'I've found that, as the author Jim Collins suggests, a useful point of reference is to look at how a trial lawyer prepares to make her case to a jury. She is very unlikely to only look at one piece of evidence. She will probably discuss a number of different issues in the opposition's case. Any single element is unlikely to convince the jury to decide in her client's favour. But, taken as a cluster of facts and ideas, the lawyer can build a credible case that helps people believe her. That's really what any good salesperson does too, rather than rely on just one "silver bullet" measured fact.'

'Yes, I'd never thought of it like that. But, what I really want to know is, how do you do it? What do you say?'

'Well, I know that Mark has several useful techniques, but they all stem from repeatedly asking yourself this question: "What could I possibly say or do to help someone feel that our solution works?"

"What could I possibly say or do to help someone feel that our solution works?"

'The great thing about asking yourself questions is that your brain is surprisingly resourceful in finding answers. The knack most people don't have is to ask yourself a *helpful* question, and to ask it in a spirit of positive expectation, rather than doubt.

'And when I ask this question of myself or of a colleague who is involved in delivering the service, sooner or later we always find answers.

'The first kind of answer I usually get is *stories*. That is, in your case, examples of specific patients whose lives improved because of your hospice.

'These are going to be the classic *before* and *after* stories, whereby someone had a particular challenge, but your charity did something to make it better, and it worked. My guess is that in the last couple of weeks you've heard several of these.'

'Yes, I heard three or four like that. One of the ones I really liked was from Viv, our head of adult services, who told me about one elderly patient called Clive with prostate cancer who had been on a busy ward in hospital for three weeks. He didn't have any family to visit him and quite apart from his physical condition, which was getting worse and worse, he was absolutely miserable. Because he was barely eating he had lost more than two stone and felt like he was fading away.

'So he was sent to Alice House because he was dying, and Viv remembers that the day he arrived Clive told her that all he wanted now was to die.

'So Viv told me that she and her team laid on the usual Alice House all round treatment, by which she meant helping him not just medically, but also emotionally, socially and psychologically. As an example, his room had a view of one of the rose gardens, so he could look at the flowers, sunshine and the wildlife, which was in stark contrast to what he'd been staring at in the huge third floor hospital ward next to Archway underground. And a big thing was that he was visited by our volunteers, a couple of whom he got on really well with, because he said they could banter with him about football and motorbikes. Not only that, he got his appetite back, which believe me is a lot easier when you're offered three home-cooked meals a day, made by a chef who comes to your bedside to find out your favourite foods, and will even send out for fish and chips if that's what it takes to tempt you to eat.

'Well, it turns out that after a couple of weeks of home-cooked food and meaningful human interaction, Clive felt quite a bit better, to the point that not only did he not die, but – and this is the bit I could barely believe when Viv told me – he was even well enough to go home! Now he still comes in for day hospice care once a week, but he goes home in the afternoon … and he's still going strong in good spirits most of the time, and this is five months after he said all he wanted was to die.'

As Claire finished, there was a pause. Her two companions had been listening intently.

Nila broke the silence. 'Claire, there is nothing you could tell us about Alice House that is more persuasive than what you just said. Mark will, I'm sure, offer some other ways to convey impact, but to just seek out specific, real examples like this and be able to pass them on to the right people at the right time … this, to me, is the heart of great fundraising.'

· THE FOURTH LAW ·
THE LAW OF
CONTRAST
—

THE MOST CERTAIN
WAY TO HELP SOMEONE
WANT TO GIVE IS TO
EVOKE A PROBLEM
THEY CARE ABOUT
AND THEN HELP THEM
BELIEVE YOUR CHARITY
IS ABLE TO SOLVE IT.

—

CHAPTER 8

Impact

Nila had had to get away to what she'd described as a 'boring but unavoidable' internal meeting. Mark and Claire had thanked her and said goodbye.

'Have you had lunch yet?' asked Mark.

'No, I had to rush straight here.' Suddenly Claire felt really hungry.

Opposite the sky-scraper they found a coffee shop and bought baguettes. They were sitting near the counter. The staff were working hard, shouting out orders. Claire loved the smell and the energy of a good coffee shop.

Mark asked what she thought of Nila's advice. Claire remembered how the story about Clive had helped them see the extraordinary difference great hospice care can make. It had been exhilarating to see the impact that this specific, real example had made on her listeners. She realised that if you had enough rapport to tell a story like this, it would go some way to helping them believe that donations make a difference.

'Well, it's really powerful. I really hadn't considered that the two most important things to do are to evoke the problem and then help people feel that it works. I now realise that what I used to do was just talk as sensibly as I could about the hospice, and hope that the other person wouldn't ask any difficult questions.

'But what you and Nila showed me today is a much more precise, considered way of working out what would help the donor decide to help.'

'That's right. Now, even people who have understood that *the problem* and *effectiveness at solving it*, are the two most important concepts to convey … well, even those people usually

> 'I now realise that what I used to do was just talk as sensibly as I could about the hospice, and hope that the other person wouldn't ask any difficult questions.'

fail to influence because what they say, or for that matter, write, is too abstract.

'The reason you helped us feel the power of hospice care was because your example about Clive was tangible, and it was also so clearly true. Very few fundraisers do this because they haven't in advance collected the specific stories and worked out how to use them to achieve the right influencing objective.'

'Yes, I see that now. But unless you knew all this, you wouldn't, would you? There's so much pressure to do other work that this level of thought and preparation isn't going to happen unless you really decide to make time for it.'

Chewing his baguette, Mark nodded.

'But there are a couple of things still bothering me … for one thing, what if you work for a charity where there aren't any stories? I mean, although until two weeks ago I hadn't been making use of them, I think I'm pretty lucky for stories in a hospice, because I work in the same building as the patients. But what if you raise funds for somewhere that doesn't really have stories? And secondly, I know James touched on this but, stories aren't the only way of conveying impact, are they? Surely facts and figures are really important as well?'

Mark nodded again and finished his mouthful. 'They're both good questions. Let's answer them in order. People often ask me this first question if they work for a research charity, or a school or university. Is that what you mean?'

'Yes, or even an arts organisation like a gallery or a museum. I mean, if they decide to improve a gallery space, I don't see that there's a story.'

'This is such an important misconception, let me be clear. After two decades of working with more than two thousand not-for-profit organisations of every kind, here's what I have found. There are *always* stories. If there were no stories then your charity's services, scholarships or exhibitions don't work and your charity doesn't deserve to raise a penny anyway.'

Mark's tone softened as he continued, 'Usually, what people really mean when they ask this question is "What if I don't currently have any stories, because stories are hard to get hold of for our organisation?" This is a more intelligent question because, can you see that it takes back your power to take action?

'And the first part of my answer is thank goodness we've realised we need stories, and they are out there somewhere, even if they aren't on a plate for us and we may need to show a little determination to get them. And, while we're seeing the silver lining, thank goodness the charity needed to recruit someone smart and proactive like me, rather than getting by with some robot with no initiative.

'Now, maybe achieving this involves overcoming some organisational politics in order to set up a skype conversation with your colleague who is thousands of miles away where the emergency supplies are being distributed; or perhaps it means making time to regularly walk into the museum's exhibition space and talk to the members of the public or the teachers and children who are benefiting from your museum. Or, for the first type of story, the one that evokes the problem, who could you talk to who is missing out because the current gallery is not good enough for access, or light, or space ... I mean, if there's nothing wrong with the current exhibition space, your museum doesn't need a new one, and if that's how you really feel, then go and work for a museum that does have a genuine problem to solve.'

'And, while we're seeing the silver lining, thank goodness the charity needed to recruit someone smart and proactive like me, rather than getting by with some robot with no initiative.'

Claire had not thought about it in this way before. 'Yes, I get all that. The stories are always there. But how about for a research charity tackling a complex disease, where the scientists are clear that they're nowhere near a cure, and even the optimistic ones would say the progress will take decades, not years?'

'Well, what do you think?'

'Hmmm. I suppose that for the stories that show what the problem is ... there should be plenty of stories which demonstrate the problem, because you're doing the research to stop this kind of suffering. There are probably thousands of those stories, if you look for them. My guess is some research charities wouldn't instinctively understand the value of those examples, because those patients have not been helped by your research, but I think Nila would find some real examples of people whose situations show particular aspects of the disease, such as the way it affects your immune system, and the consequences of that, or for instance how current treatments cause certain painful side effects.'

Mark continued, 'And, for the impact stories, that may seem harder, but in most cases, the research your charity is carrying out is probably far beyond square one on the journey of understanding. Unless your charity is brand new, your charity's researchers must have made some progress in understanding or treating this disease. It means bringing to life any steps along the research journey that have been achieved so far.'

Claire was scribbling lots of notes. Mark waited for her to finish her sentence, before adding 'And as I say, we shouldn't only look inwards. The more global your mind-set, i.e. framing this as humanity, rather than a British charity trying to understand and cure this disease, you start to realise there are two more options. One is, "what has any researcher, even if not funded by your charity, ever achieved to make progress with this disease?" That example can help answer the question "does research into this disease make a difference?"

'And secondly, it's sometimes useful to look even more broadly. Sometimes a donor really needs to be convinced that research, that is, *invest now for improvement over the medium or long-term*, pays off. So find examples that show this to be true. For instance, in the 1950s, a child diagnosed with leukaemia had a devastatingly slim chance of surviving – roughly nine out of every ten children would die. In under thirty years, those survival rates rocketed up from one in ten to where they are now, which is nine out of ten children surviving.'

'So you would say that to a donor even if you worked for a different kind of research charity?'

'It would definitely be an option. You see, knowing that extraordinary success story for the power of donating to medical research completely changes the frame through which we then look at your charity's research plans. If you help your audience focus on this, and consider the many thousands of children, teenagers and adults alive today because leukaemia is no longer a death sentence … I think they will feel differently about the time frame your charity operates in, and they will be more likely to believe that research into this other disease will pay off.'

'Yes I get it.' But something else was troubling Claire. She asked, 'Okay, this is all really helpful stuff. But obviously "story" is not the only way of conveying impact. I see how useful tangible examples are, but what's your view on finding ways to show the charity's effectiveness numerically?'

'Well, if you're lucky, there may be a strong measurable outcome that gives a sense that hospice care works. Just occasionally this is very clear, like a fundraiser I met last week who's raising funds for a piece of hospital equipment. Apparently, if you undergo this kidney operation at the moment, it's a very invasive procedure and so it takes at least seven days in hospital to recover … and you can see that that is bad for the patient's health, as well as being very expensive. Well, my client

'In under thirty years, those survival rates rocketed up from one in ten to where they are now, which is nine out of ten children surviving.'

is raising money to pay for a fantastic high-tech machine which will make the operation so precise that the patient will be able to go home the same day as the operation.'

'Wow! That's extraordinary. I don't think there's anything as extreme as that that we can say for hospice care.'

'No, probably nothing that cut and dried, but that's okay. I like what Tom Peters has to say about this. He writes that some things that are very important in life are extremely difficult to measure numerically. I'm talking about valuable charitable aims, like retaining a sense of human dignity because a patient feels treated like a person, or peace of mind because they no longer have to worry about financial problems because Alice House's counselling and advice service helped them sort things out. As I understand it, feeling like you matter, and peace of mind – these are important things for a hospice to aim to help with. But none of them can very well be conveyed numerically.'

Claire had an idea. She asked 'Well, how about the fact that the ratio of nurses to patients in most hospitals is around one nurse to at least nine patients, whereas at Alice House every nurse can devote their attention to looking after just one or two patients?'

'That's really strong and it helps us build a case. But, strictly speaking, these ratios are not an outcome in the sense of some improved state or result for the patient, so much as the vehicle by which improvements would be achieved. Do you see the difference?'

'Yes, I do. And it seems obvious when you think about it this way. Well, I wonder if we already track patient wellness in some way. There probably is some way of putting a number on this, even if it's imperfect. If there is any kind of feedback form that the patient or maybe the spouse fills in, it would be good to know the percentage that rated their experience of care in the hospice as excellent. My gut feeling based on conversations with people so far is that that number would be really high. And crucially, if someone at a trust or company had never visited Alice House, they would never guess at how sky high those satisfaction rates or improvements in wellness would be.'

'Yes, that would certainly be a useful piece in the jigsaw.'

'You know, I'm sure there is something we could find if we talk to our head of care and tell her the sort of thing we'd like to be able to convey. So what else could I use to build this case? To be honest, once I get people to come to Alice House the atmosphere and the people are so amazing that it kind of sells itself.'

'I bet that's true. Yes, I think a lot of your challenge, when you meet potential supporters in their own offices is to find a way to get them to be sufficiently interested that they agree to visit the hospice.

'I can't remember, I know James mentioned social proof, but did he also talk about one of Cialdini's other weapons of influence, the one about invoking authority?'

Claire looked pleased. 'No, he didn't, but I read some demonstrations of how powerful it is in Cialdini's *The Small BIG* which James gave me.'

'You've read it, have you?'

'No, but I am half way through … in fact, you were right, if you just keep it in your bag when you're commuting you can read three or four chapters a week without investing any extra time at home. I used to fritter away so much time when I was commuting so I love this habit. But anyway, how do you use *authority* to help people trust that your charity works?'

'Well, you know that people attach far more credibility to ideas when they are stated by figures of authority, such as the judges of competitions or head teachers or academics with PhDs. To use this, we need to find someone who thinks that what our charity does is really effective, and whose name would carry gravitas with our listener.'

'Like, maybe, a doctor.'

'Well, maybe, especially if it's clear to the listener that they're independent of the hospice. I'd be most influenced by anyone external, like a chief medical officer, or some kind of inspector.'

'Yes, that makes sense. I'm sure I can find something … but there's another thing that's confusing … In all of this, I still haven't said anything about how the hospice care is actually delivered. We've answered "Does it work?" without answering "How does it work?" That doesn't make sense to me.'

'Well, actually you have. Through your story, you told me quite a bit about how you provide such holistic, dedicated social and emotional care, like the power of the Alice House volunteers and the home-cooked food, to lift people's spirits. And things like this are not unimportant. They're just not *as important* as the results, like Paul becoming so well that he no longer wanted to die and he even became well enough to go home.

'But on the subject of *how* you make this wonderful difference, that is, if you are to talk about the service itself, my advice is to know what your "special sauce" is.'

Claire looked faintly amused. 'What's that?'

'Well, you've probably heard of USPs, or unique selling points.'

She nodded.

'Well, the special sauce is similar, but when I search for the special sauce, it stops me listing six or seven bullet point USPs and helps me focus on the one or two key reasons which make our way of delivering this service especially good. What makes your day hospice care so great?'

'Well, it depends. But quite a few of our patients don't have a car. So for one thing, our transport team come and get you from your home to bring you to the hospice each time. And for some people this takes away a major obstacle to attending, as well as removing all the stress of waiting at bus stops in all weathers or the hassle of trying to arrange lifts with neighbours.

'Very good,' said Mark. 'So this idea of getting clear on the special sauce helps you to say only your strongest USPs, the ones that are most likely to frame your service in a positive light.

'Actually, the ideas that Nila and I have given you today are not an exhaustive list of how to apply the law of contrast. They're a pretty useful, systematic start, to prevent you talking in a way that is unpersuasive. But the most important thing for any area of work that is important to your potential supporters, is to ask yourself, how could I help them feel, firstly the problem and, secondly that our way of solving it works?'

They had finished their baguettes and Claire realised she had to get back to the office if she was going to make the phone calls she'd planned for that afternoon.

Claire thanked Mark warmly, and made her way back to Alice House.

CHAPTER 9

The magic formula

laire managed to make her phone calls and made a point of feeling good that two of the calls had resulted in meetings with people who might at some point want to become company partners with Alice House.

When she got home she was weary, but again her head was buzzing with the implications of what she had learned.

She started to unload the dishwasher and thought about not only the things she had heard that day, but also about everything else she had learned since the conference in July. She now understood that the principles complemented each other, adding up to more than the sum of each part.

'So I wonder why couldn't he have told me all the laws from the start?'

She continued to put the clean cutlery away.

And as she did so, she knew the answer. The discussions she had had today wouldn't have been nearly so powerful if she hadn't already gone and found those specific examples about the hospice for herself.

By the time she'd eaten it was after nine o clock, but she decided to turn off the TV and write up her notes from the day's conversations.

She started by dividing ideas about persuasive messages into two sections, following the law of contrast.

1. Ideas to help someone understand/feel/focus on the problem.

2. Ideas to help someone feel (and believe) that your charity's solution (e.g. service) works.

Based on the notes she had jotted down, she then wrote down the following:

THE MAGIC FORMULA FOR FINDING PERSUASIVE THINGS TO SAY

1) Ideas to help someone understand/feel/focus on the problem.

  a) What is the essence of the problem faced by our patients (and their families)?

  b) What is not obvious about this problem?

  c) What story or example brings to life how difficult this can be?

2) Ideas to help someone feel (and believe) that your charity's solution (e.g. service) works.

  a) What story shows that this aspect of our hospice works?

  b) Can you find any way to show the impact numerically?

  c) How could you apply Cialdini's six weapons of influence, for example, authority or social proof, to help someone believe in the effectiveness of your service?

  d) What, simply put, is this service, and what is Alice House's secret sauce?!

Claire realised that if Nila and Mark were right, she could use the questions to systematically work out persuasive ways of talking about the three or four services or topics her supporters were most likely to find motivating. But the first step was to get clear on what those most common topics were. She wrote:

The in-patient (i.e. residential care) service at Alice House

The day hospice care service.

The counselling and advice to patients and families service.

She set herself the challenge of finding persuasive ideas on the subject of the day hospice care unit, using her questions, in just twenty minutes. By 9.45 she stopped to read through her notes. She knew it wasn't finished, but she'd made an excellent start. Where her answers were weak, she at least noted down ideas for where to seek out the relevant story, measured outcome or fact.

She was so amazed at the power of what she'd done that she switched her attention to the counselling and advice service and started the process of answering the questions again. It was past 10.00 by the time she had a written rough notes for this one too, and she was getting tired.

And a quick look at Alice House's key service, that is, provision of ongoing residential care to patients, revealed that this was actually made up of many different elements that were vital, but clearly needed a lot of funding to operate. She set herself the challenge of initially splitting her notes on this large topic into discrete sections, such as nursing, volunteers, and food and drink to see if it might help her organise her ideas.

Claire decided it was now too late to start work on any of these sections, but she decided on a time later in the week when she would write Magic Formula ideas about the Nursing section. And then, pleased with her progress, she put her notes away.

CHAPTER 10

The **FIFTH** law

I t was late afternoon and over a month had passed since Claire's visit to Jardines Bank. The warmth of late summer had been replaced by blustery October winds and several days of persistent rain. And yet Claire was in good spirits as she waited in the refreshment area of a training venue in North London. Today was the day of her final meeting with Mark.

He had invited her to meet one of his friends who he said owed much of her success to her mastery of the fifth law.

The course in training room 3 finished and the attendees said their goodbyes and left. As the last couple of people packed up their things, Claire went to say hello to Mark. He was looking tired, but brightened when he saw her. Soon he was introducing her to a woman who was not making preparations to leave.

'Claire, this is Laura,' he said. 'She's one of the results coaches that support the fundraisers who attend my *Major Gifts Mastery Programme*.'

'Pleased to finally meet you, Claire. How's it all going?'

They sat down around a table in the training room and Claire told them the highs and lows of the journey she'd been on over the past few months. She'd made immense progress.

She told them she now had a default plan for how to conduct any meeting or informal pitch, and she was far more confident talking to supporters than she ever had been, in large part because through the law of firepower she had sought out far more persuasive, tangible things to say. Not only this, but she'd used the law of understanding to first appreciate who she was talking to, and the law of contrast to combine her stories and ideas into persuasive arguments about most of the topics that might be motivating. She only spoke about elements of the hospice that might appeal to who she was talking to. And yet ...

'And yet, for all the great conversations I've been having and the progress I'm making,' she explained, 'something still isn't quite working sometimes. And whatever that something is, I'm sure it's the reason people don't say 'yes' when I invite them to consider a gift or a partnership'.

'What do you think it might be?' asked Mark.

'I can't say for sure. But I think the problem is deep down, I don't quite see why anyone would give this much money away or even go to all the hassle it takes to set up a company partnership. Obviously our patients need Alice House's services, and obviously some of these potential donors could afford to give if they wanted to … but how do you persuade someone to give away say, half a million or even £5,000 of their own money? I know it happens, but at the same time … I can't quite get my head around it.'

'And this,' said Mark, 'is where Laura comes in.' He told her that Laura was a fundraising manager for a large public gallery in Edinburgh. In the fundraising community in Scotland she had a reputation for being able to develop warm relationships with the wealthiest and supposedly spikiest donors, helping them enjoy giving generously to the various causes she had represented in her fifteen year career. The gallery she worked for had so far raised £32 million of the total £45 million target, one year into the three year public phase of the Appeal.

'So tell us, Laura,' said Mark, 'what do you think is the key to influencing the people you meet?'

Laura looked at Claire and pursed her lips. 'Well, what I had always known at some level, but that Mark helped me see more clearly a few years ago, is this. What you say is important, but *how* you say it, and indeed your overall state, *the energy* you carry, is even more important in whether or not people say yes to you.'

This seemed to make sense. 'Sure, I get that, and there are times I can just tell I'm much more confident and somehow more persuasive than other times. But what can we do about the times when we're not? Doesn't it just come with experience?'

'Clearly experience can help, but do you want to wait five or ten years to feel bullet-proof confidence when you ask a donor to consider making a gift? Or as you did with Mark's other techniques for speeding up progress, do you want to be able to change how you feel in a matter of moments?

Claire grinned. The outrageous claim was contrary to everything she'd ever been told about the elusive business of confidence. But she'd found that everything Mark and his friends had told her so far, *when she actually applied it,* had turned out to be far more powerful than she had imagined.

'I think I'd like to know the fast route.'

'Good,' said Laura, 'then here goes. The fifth law is the law of state.

This law asserts that the greatest factor in our ability to influence is our state.'

The fifth law - the law of state
'The greatest factor in our ability to influence is our state.'

'Most people act as though your states or moods just happen to you. The truth is that we are affecting what states we will experience, either consciously or unconsciously, all the time. I imagine that in explaining some of the other laws, Mark will have mentioned some of the ideas of Tony Robbins. Well then, as you may know, one thing he specialises in is helping elite performers in business, sport, show business, in fact people who excel in any field, to achieve a peak level of performance when they really need it. And in order to help people in this way, he makes use of the three fundamental ways we can influence how we feel: what things mean to us, what we focus our attention on, and our physiology.

'If we take responsibility for any of these, we can affect how we feel, how we behave, and the energy we project. If we take responsibility for all three, we can make a big shift in our state and a huge improvement in the results we experience every day.

The power of choosing what things mean

'Let's start with meaning, which is to say that what you allow any situation or event to mean to you is very important. And what something means to you is another way of saying what you believe about it.

'Whenever I've met people who achieve extraordinary fundraising results, I've found they share this belief: donors gain massively from giving to a cause they care about, or at least they can potentially gain massively.'

'Do you mean in terms of getting a plaque with their name on it on the new building, or a company looking good to its customers?'

'Well, to some extent I mean that ... I've found that many human beings can benefit in these ways for being generous. And I don't discount the importance of those.

'But more, I mean that anyone can gain psychologically from the act of giving. Emotionally, and indeed some would say spiritually, people feel better through giving to a cause they care about.

'...think of any volunteering you've ever done. In addition to some camaraderie that the volunteering gave you, it probably also just felt good to be contributing.'

'If you don't believe me, think of any volunteering you've ever done. In addition to some camaraderie that the volunteering gave you, it probably also just felt good to be contributing. And if you have never done any formal volunteering, then think of any time you've done a good turn for someone when you didn't need to. In fact, no one would have known if you hadn't helped that neighbour or that elderly person struggling in the railway station. When you think about it, even though you probably did these things because "it was the right thing to do", you nevertheless felt good.

This all made sense to Claire. There was a time she'd volunteered to read for a blind student at university and, although sometimes difficult, it had usually given her a surprisingly warm glow.

'I understand what you're talking about. But aren't we just talking about the various motivations that donors have? What's the difference, Mark, between what Laura is explaining here, and what you told me about how to first understand a potential donor before starting to say anything detailed about my hospice?'

'Good question. The two ideas are related, but the reason Laura is explaining this now is entirely different. Of course we need to understand something of the other person's interests if we're to influence them. But what Laura is doing now does not concern the specifics of any particular reason why an individual may feel good to give. Instead, we are focusing on the deeper and more fundamental truth that to give, to contribute at all, is good for the *giver*. This is not about helping you choose what to say, but about emboldening you to feel a bullet-proof confidence whenever you invite people to support at all.'

> 'Instead, we are focusing on the deeper and more fundamental truth that to give, to contribute at all, is good for the *giver*'

Mark paused. Claire seemed to see the difference.

So he asked, 'Do you think that the way we say things makes a difference as to how people will react?'

Claire smiled, remembering her mate Sinead who could make the same suggestion as any of her other friends, but say it with such certainty that people invariably said yes.

'Yes, it makes a huge difference. I think that's what most of my problem has been lately. It's that I've not been remotely sure that they're going to want to actually support, so even if I ask them with words that are confident, they're never going to say 'yes'.

'But what can I do about it? I've known the big donation would be good for the hospice and the patients, but at some level I've felt the donor would be losing out if they chose to give that much. But if I did what I think you're saying, I think I'd come across as pushy. I hate the idea that I could come across as pushy.'

'And happily,' said Laura, 'you don't have to be pushy. All you need to do is switch your focus from you (or even from your beneficiaries) to the donor, and make sure you've got perfectly clear what it means to offer someone the chance to give to a cause they care about.

'I've observed that when very successful fundraisers go to invite someone to consider making a large gift, they feel they're taking a wonderful opportunity, or offer, to that person. In that sense, they don't feel it's an "ask" at all.

'So assuming that like me, you can see that this belief they have is one of the main reasons they're so successful, then all you need to do is see if you can believe the same thing.'

'But I already do believe giving is good for people ... or at least I think I do.' Claire's voice tailed off.

'Yes, and I've found that most fundraisers believe this idea, at least in principle. It's just that when the pressure is on because, for example, you have to phone that person for the third time and her assistant seemed blunt with you last time ... or you have to ask her to give your hospice £10,000 ... on those occasions, much of the reason many fundraisers either fail to pick up the phone, or fail ask for the gift with absolute confidence, is that in that moment they are not focusing on the truth that their offer to the donor is in the donor's interests.'

'Okay, this makes sense in theory. I just don't know how to do it in practice.'

'Well, in his book *Awaken the Giant Within*, Tony Robbins suggests the following: he says an idea is like a table top lying flat on the floor, with nothing to hold it up. To make a table top stand up, place strong table legs underneath it. And if you want to turn a valuable idea into a strong conviction that will help you, then all you have to do is prop up that idea. What props up a belief? Any reference, any example that you already have that is consistent with that belief.'

Claire didn't follow.

Laura continued, 'So if anyone wants to be confident when approaching donors or asking them for money, the first step is to find references that are consistent with the idea that giving is good for you. Can you think of any ideas or evidence that backs up the idea that giving is psychologically good for the giver?'

Initially Claire couldn't think, but then she remembered a recent stewardship phone call she'd made to a donor. She told them about Mrs Davies, a wealthy supporter who had given £5,000 to the hospice. When Claire called to thank Mrs Davies, the supporter had said quite sincerely that it really was her pleasure and in fact, she had thanked Claire for providing this chance for her and her husband 'to give something back'.

'So if anyone wants to be confident when approaching donors or asking them for money, the first step is to find references that are consistent with the idea that giving is good for you.'

Mark's eyes lit up. 'And this is the crux,' he said. 'Do you think Mrs Davies' emotions and indeed her life, are worse, the same or better, as a result of her making this donation to your hospice?'

'Well yes, she certainly gave me the impression that giving that money made her happy.'

Now Claire understood. She realised that almost everyone who helped Alice House – the supporters, donors and volunteers – may well give their time or money for kind reasons, but they still were all gaining something from the arrangement in a psychological sense. And this truth in no way diminished the generosity of what they did. It was merely a happy side effect.

But then a thought occurred to Claire. She was thinking of Colin Noon, Alice House's most notoriously grumpy supporter. He seemed not to be remotely happy, or at least if he was, he hid it extremely well.

'Are you saying that giving *always* makes people happier?'

'No', said Mark. 'I'm saying I believe that giving has the potential to be good for people, to meet some fundamental human needs, which is why many of them get positively addicted to doing generous things with their time, their money, or both. Certainly, some may not show this benefit openly. And I'm saying that even if sometimes it doesn't always work out that way, the belief that in general this is true is the most empowering mind-set to adopt if you want massive success as a fundraiser.

'The reason it's so necessary to understand this idea is that some donors you meet will be unaware that giving is good for you. They're likely to see charity as something that we do out of duty, or concern for others, without ever being aware that it can have a positive impact on the giver. And since they're not aware of it, we have to be certain that this is true. Another of Tony Robbins' ideas that I've found helpful is that "when there is rapport, the person who is more certain of something, over time, influences the other".

> 'So the more certain we are that it is in the supporters' own interests to agree to meet us or make a donation, the easier it will be to help them want to do these things.'

'So the more certain we are that it is in the supporters' own interests to agree to meet us or make a donation, the easier it will be to help them want to do these things.'

Claire liked this idea. She said, 'Okay, I think I get this in theory now … and even just thinking about it has helped me. But I think it must be harder to do in practice than you make it sound. What I'd like to know, Laura, is how you became so confident asking people for money?'

'Well firstly I examined what I really believed about the fundraising process. Then I got rid of the beliefs that were actually *charity win – donor lose*, by seeking out ideas which reinforced a more helpful belief about what it means to offer someone the chance to give. If I were you, I'd collect notes of any evidence that helps you feel this to be true. So for example, you could go on YouTube and watch clips of *The Secret Millionaire* programme, where the wealthy person is always happier after giving away lots of money; you could deliberately find specific occasions in your own life when you did something generous with your time or your money and which had a similar effect on you. The more you focus on evidence that supports this idea, the easier it will be to automatically feel confident when the pressure is on.

'But there is something else which has really helped me to create the happy career I now enjoy. But before I tell you this second element, I have to say that I'm running low on energy.'

The power of controlling your focus

They went out to the café area. As they made their drinks and found a plate of biscuits, Laura carried on.

'The second element is related to meaning, but it's the idea of changing your focus. We must be so careful what we focus our attention on, because what we focus on, we feel.

'If we leave it to chance, the dominant question in our head before and during a high pressure meeting

'We must be so careful what we focus our attention on, because what we focus on, we feel.'

tends to be something like "How can I not mess this up?" or "How can I get him to open up?" or even "How can I get him to give?" Although these questions are entirely understandable, none of them is helpful.'

'I see that not wanting to mess up might make you more likely to make a mistake,' said Claire, 'but what's wrong with wanting the donor to open up or to give?'

'The problem with these questions is that when you look closely, you realise that they are focused on your needs, on the things that will be good for *you*. And as such, whereas they may sometimes seem to work, the other person often feels manipulated to do something that may not be in their best interests. If you think of the idea we've just been talking about, what do you think might be a better question we could ask ourselves as we go into a meeting with a supporter?'

Claire thought for a moment. 'Well, you could ask "How could I help this person enjoy today's meeting?" or "How could I help her enjoy finding out things to do with our charity's cause that she cares about?"'

'Now you've got it. Can you see how differently we would feel and act going into a meeting where either of these was the dominant focus of our attention? If this is the main intention in our nervous system, then everything we do will be more positive, more generous-spirited and that shift will help us feel far more confident.'

'And what about asking for money? You're not going to tell me I shouldn't plan that the donor should make a donation?'

'No, at the appropriate stage in a supporter's relationship with our charity, by all means we should plan how we might make an offer that's likely to succeed. It's just that rather than "How could I get him to give?" which is what 97% of fundraisers say and think in approaching this situation, I would go into that meeting focusing on the question "How could I help him want to give generously today, if appropriate?"'

'But is it really this simple? Asking yourself a question?'

'Well what is thinking, if not a series of questions which we are asking and answering all day long? I grant you, most of us do it unconsciously, but I really believe that this is what thinking consists of. So the most sure-fire way to change your focus is to deliberately ask yourself a more helpful question, rather than allowing free rein to the default questions we've been conditioned to ask automatically.'

'This is really helpful. The two ideas make sense to me. When I think of a fundraising conversation as something that's in the interests of the potential donor, I see that not only is it true, but also that it would massively help how I feel about the whole game. And also I see that if I set my focus by asking "How could I help this person today?" it will help me be at my generous best, rather than on the defensive. But what if I'm already feeling anxious? I'm not sure I'll be able to remember to think in this way.'

> 'I would go into that meeting focusing on the question "How could I help him want to give generously today, if appropriate?"'

'Well for one thing, the more you practise the meaning and the focus every day, rather than only try to apply them on the day of an important meeting with a donor, that will help because you'll have conditioned it. The neural pathways in your brain for this way of thinking will have become stronger and so easier to activate. But there is something else, the third leg of the stool which supports any desirable state that you want. And this is the most powerful and under-used tool of the lot.'

Mark pointed to his watch and Laura checked the time. She frowned and quickly drained her cup.

She said, 'I'm so sorry Claire, but if I don't leave for the airport very soon I'll miss my flight home. So if you want to find out about the third secret to unstoppable confidence when asking people to donate, it's going to be Mark who shows you the final piece of the puzzle.'

Claire thanked Laura for her help, and once she'd gone, Mark looked her in the eye.

The power of physiology

'Okay, you want the third key to feeling confident with donors and companies? This is my favourite. I'm talking of course, about what you do with your physiology'.

'Physiology? You mean my body language?'

'Well, I tend not to say "body language" because to most people that implies the messages that our bodies send to other people. Instead, I say physiology because although what the other person sees does influence how they perceive you, it is not the main reason why taking responsibility for your physiology is so important.

'If you want to feel good states or emotions, like happy, confident or in control, then the quickest way to achieve them is not through focus or meaning, but by making a big shift in what you do with your body.

'But it's much more powerful to actually do it, rather than just talk or read about it. Are you up for a little experiment?' asked Mark.

Claire looked dubious. 'Sure.'

'Okay, slump down in your chair like this … now look down, like I'm doing … Okay, and now put your hand on your neck like this.'

Claire copied him. As she did so, she felt uncomfortable to be doing something that was unnatural. But then, beyond the awkwardness, she felt a much stronger feeling. She felt a heaviness, a lethargy, verging on melancholy.

'How about a sigh?' said Mark, and he let out a long, slow sigh. He was still looking down.

Claire did the same, copying Mark's way of looking down, dropping her chin towards her chest and slumping her shoulders.

'How are you feeling?' he said after about twenty seconds.

'Terrible ... I feel on-the-way-to-unhappy ... I don't ... I don't really have any energy,' said Claire, amazed at the strength of the feeling she had just manufactured.

'On a scale of one to ten, negative to positive, what score would you give this feeling?'

'I'd give it a two or three. Yes, it's possible to feel worse, but two or three out of ten is about right.'

'Okay, so now do what I do.' And with that, Mark sprang up out of his chair and stood up straight.

Bemused, Claire did the same.

'Put your feet shoulder width apart, like this. No wider ... that's it.'

She frowned. Mark added, 'Even if that doesn't feel natural or normal, it's really important in this exercise to put them shoulder width apart, so you literally have a solid base. Then, shoulders back. That's it. Chin a bit higher, that's it.'

He pointed to his sternum in the centre of his chest. 'Imagine you could raise your sternum by half a centimetre higher than you normally would. Now some slower, deeper breaths ... and now finally add a big, cheesy grin,' and as he did so, he allowed a huge smile to appear, showing his teeth.

Claire did the same. As she did so, she felt ridiculous. This was not normal behaviour. She pushed on anyway, because 'normal' behaviour had so far failed to get her what she wanted. And as she let go of the feeling of embarrassment in occupying someone else's posture, she was taken aback by how different she felt.

'That's good. Great in fact. So now, if you were to describe how you feel, what would you say?'

Claire's smile had become genuine. 'Well, I feel ... more buoyant, I mean, as well as a certain

This was not normal behaviour. She pushed on anyway, because 'normal' behaviour had so far failed to get her what she wanted oddness, because I don't normally do this … I do feel strangely happy, and sort of, sort of in control, as if I'm less frantic … it's as if somehow I've got more poise.'

'Interesting. What number out of ten would you give this state?'

'I'd have to say at least an eight.'

'Okay, so let's sit down,' but he was noticeably sitting up that bit taller, taking up that bit more space than he had been earlier. Claire followed suit.

'So, what did you learn?'

'Well, changing what you do with your body has a much bigger impact on how you feel than I ever realised. What's most weird is there wasn't a new reason to feel good. I hadn't just received good news. The only thing that changed was artificial. And yet it worked. I want to say that I always knew this … but actually, that wouldn't be true. I mean, I've always tried to be confident, but the truth is, last week when I was on my way to meet a donor, I was quite worried about how the meeting would go. And I tried to stop worrying by talking myself out of it. But the more I tried to talk myself out of the anxiety, the worse I felt.'

'So, knowing what you know now, what would you do next time?'

'I guess I'd force myself to change what I was doing with my posture, my breathing and my face, even if it felt initially a bit false to smile when I was feeling so unconfident. I'd stand up and walk, or maybe even strut, on my way there, and that would help me access feelings more like these.'

'Right, and here's the trick. If that was the only thing you did, then you would do far better in your meetings, but it probably would be hard to sustain.

'The truth is that when you're doing the more confident and happy physiology, changing your focus and giving the meeting a different meaning becomes way easier,…'

But remember the other two ingredients Laura told you. The truth
is that when you're doing the more confident and happy physiology,
changing your focus and giving the meeting a different meaning
becomes way easier, because your body and brain become more open
to those ways of thinking.'

'But why is that?'

'Well, the best explanation that I ever had was in a TED talk I
watched on-line. It's from a professor called Amy Cuddy of Harvard
Business School. I honestly think it was the most useful twenty-one
minutes I've ever spent on-line.'

'What's it called?' said Claire, reaching for her pen.

'I'm not sure, but if you Google "Amy Cuddy body posture" you'll
find it. The thing is, I had already been taught how to use many of the
ideas, and I'd felt the difference in practice, but I'd often struggled to
explain why such a powerful technique works. The problem, you see,
is it sounds to many people like some lame positive thinking cliché, so
I'd always struggled to show people with a down-to-earth mind-set,
why this is such an effective way to change how you feel and therefore
what you're able to do.

'Here's what Dr Cuddy did. She had groups of people adopt various
poses, and then measured how they felt, how they behaved and what
was going on with the hormones in their blood.

'This is the fascinating bit for me. She took saliva samples from all
the participants, before and after they had performed the poses, and
she was interested in two hormones in particular – testosterone and
cortisol.

'You've probably heard of testosterone, and it's usually associated
with aggression, body building and alpha males. But the fact is,
testosterone is important in both men and women in that it is the
hormone that provides all of us with feelings of inner power and
confidence. And the other one, cortisol, is linked to feelings of stress.
The more stressed you are, the more cortisol there will be in your
system.

'Can your physiology influence the mind? Everyone knows the reverse can be true, that is, our state of mind such as happy or worried, influences our facial expressions, causing us to smile or frown ... but Dr Cuddy wanted to find out whether the reverse is also true.

'So she arranged for two randomly chosen groups of people to perform what she calls "high-power poses" or "low-power poses" for only two minutes, and she took measurements before and after of both testosterone and cortisol levels using saliva samples. What Dr Cuddy found was an explanation for how a change in the body does change the mind, as well as how we feel and behave: in the people who had assumed "high-power poses", similar to what we were doing just now, testosterone increased on average by about 20%, and it decreased in the people who had been asked to do the "low-power poses" – for instance, making themselves more hunched and small and downward facing, by 10%. Not only that, but levels of the stress hormone cortisol went down in the high-power pose group by about 25% and it went up in the low-power pose people by 15%. Like you just now, neither group had received any good or bad news or been asked to think confident or unconfident thoughts.'

'Are you saying
that even if I don't
feel confident or
happy or whatever, I
should act that way
anyway, and it will
help me get better
fundraising results?'

'This is extraordinary. Are you saying that even if I don't feel confident or happy or whatever, I should act that way anyway, and it will help me get better fundraising results?'

'That's a smart question. The answer is an emphatic yes, that's exactly what Dr Cuddy's research is saying, and applying this has already helped me and Laura and the countless other fundraisers I've coached who have been disciplined enough to follow through and apply this idea. When you do, your physiology creates a self-fulfilling prophesy. It changes the way you feel, and so the way you instinctively act.'

'But you talk about power poses. You're not saying that I should go strutting into a meeting with my nose in the air? Because I don't think I could do that. And even if I could, it's not going to come across at all well with the sort of people I meet.'

'Quite right, I'm not saying you should be or act arrogant. I am saying it's essential that you don't assume the physiology of an unconfident, low-status person, even if society might presume that that is how a fundraiser should cow-tow to a powerful CEO or wealthy philanthropist. Instead, practise and get good at doing the body language of someone who is confident and high-status. Now if all you did was that, I agree, it would come across as cold or arrogant, but when you add it together with the generous focus of "How can I help this person really enjoy and get value from this meeting?" then your whole energy warms up, so that the signal you send is not arrogance but charisma, in the best sense of the word.'

As the conversation came to an end, Claire made sure she was sitting up straighter than normal, with her shoulders back and her sternum in the front of her chest a little higher. She had felt self-conscious to start with, but as she had relaxed a little while maintaining the upward energy, it had felt easier, as though she wasn't doing it for anyone else's benefit, but merely as something that made sense for her.

And as she walked back to the tube, she couldn't help but walk a little taller than had been her habit for years. And as she tried to

' "How can I help this person really enjoy and get value from this meeting?" then your whole energy warms up, so that the signal you send is not arrogance but charisma, in the best sense of the word.'

process the three ideas that Laura and Mark had explained, the most important conclusion she came to was that right now she felt good.

And it was all the more powerful to know that one reason she felt this way was that the blood flowing through her veins contained more confidence-boosting testosterone and less stress-linked cortisol than it normally would. This insight would never have occurred to her before, and to know it now felt like a secret power that had just been revealed to her.

The ideas about focus and meaning had been no less powerful, but she sensed she'd have to think them through and test what difference they made.

When Claire got home, she decided not to watch television, but to act on this exciting surge in energy. After her meal she opened her notebook and wrote down what she had learned that day.

The fifth law - the law of state
'The greatest factor in our ability to influence is our state.'

The three main ways we can influence our state are:
what we allow things to mean;
what we focus our attention and intention on;
what we do with our physiology.

Next, she opened her laptop and typed Amy Cuddy, TED, into Google. The search generated a film called 'Your body language shapes who you are'.

Sitting in a solid, upright posture, she watched the short film. She discovered that the talk added scientific depth to what Mark had already shown her and she began to understand why it had been viewed more than twenty-one million times. Apparently it was the second most viewed TED talk in history.

For one thing, she remembered that as a child, her grandmother's nagging that she should sit up straight had only made her more reluctant to bother. She decided she preferred Amy Cuddy's reasons to look after your body posture – it helps you feel confident and reduces feelings of stress.

In fact, she found it so helpful that she did something quite uncharacteristic and emailed the link to her colleagues, encouraging them to have a look.

She also looked back at her notes on Laura and Mark's table leg model. Initially she couldn't think of any more references to write in, so she stayed online and watched the last two minutes of an edition of *The Secret Millionaire*. Unequivocally, the millionaire was far happier after giving away £50,000 of her own money. Claire watched clips from a couple more episodes and the pattern recurred. She made a note of what they had said about how they felt after donating their money.

She also wanted more ideas from her own life experiences, so she decided to write a question in her notebook

What references can I possibly think of that support the idea that people gain emotionally and psychologically from giving?

Sitting on the bus the next morning, she opened her notebook and discovered several ideas and memories occurred to her without effort. As she wrote them down, she felt ever more convinced that Laura was right. 'Of course people gain psychologically when they are generous or kind without expecting something in return', she thought. 'This is human nature.' And as she did so, she realised her old apologetic hang-ups had loosened their grip. She could still understand where they came from, but they no longer eroded her eagerness to go and invite donors and companies to meet her or make a donation.

And to apply the idea of shifting her focus, she started to

deliberately ask herself questions before she went into meetings. She started with internal meetings and was taken aback by what difference it made when she focused on helping the other person, rather than what had sometimes happened in the past, which was to proactively defend herself from the start so that she wouldn't be taken advantage of.

She even tried this prior to what should have been a difficult meeting with Janice, the head of finance at Alice House. She asked herself, 'How can I help Janice to enjoy our meeting and to get the level of reassurance and information she needs, while not committing myself to unnecessary extra work?'

The effect was extraordinary. Rather than render her a pushover, Claire found she now spent far more effort on understanding what Janice really wanted. And so she discovered that what Janice actually needed was not nearly as difficult as she had feared. She had focused her energy on finding a mutually beneficial solution, rather than merely getting her excuses in early, and Janice seemed to reciprocate in wanting to understand Claire's point of view. In this trusting atmosphere, Janice turned out to be unexpectedly reasonable in offering Claire a solution to the reporting of financial information for donors, including a couple of helpful ideas that Claire would never have even known to ask for.

On reflection, Claire realised that the success of this meeting had not only stemmed from setting her intention to 'give not get', but was also probably helped by how she had been holding her body. She had specifically practised one of Cuddy's high-power poses in the toilet cubicle before the meeting, standing tall and upright, breathing calmly and smiling. She now realised that perhaps when she had tried to help others in the past, she had done so with body language that was subservient, so that she had come across as weak rather than helpful.

Buoyed up by what a difference these new tactics had made in meetings with colleagues, Claire decided to apply the ideas about meaning, focus and physiology to her next meeting with a donor.

Two weeks later, returning elated from a fantastic meeting with Graham Hunt, a partner at an accountancy firm, Claire sat at her desk and opened her notebook. She jotted down the reason she had just had three of the best donor meetings of her life was in large part thanks to the recent changes she had made. She was delighted to note that she had shifted the focus of her attention and her intention, to helping her donors have enjoyable, useful conversations with her. She sensed that the meeting the previous day may not lead to any financial support in the short term but it had nevertheless been a constructive sharing of ideas.

The other two meetings had been fantastic. On Monday, Olivia Waldron had happily agreed to make a gift of £9,000 to help fund the day hospice unit. And today, she had had an amazing meeting with Graham Hunt, in spite of his frosty reputation. He had even seemed to appreciate the chance to talk freely about his father, now in New Zealand, who was increasingly unwell. And he had also been interested to hear Claire's stories about the power of food and drink as one way to create comfort and camaraderie at Alice House.

These results were exciting enough. But even more exciting was how Claire's confidence when meeting important people, internally and externally, had been transformed. There was a lightness and optimism in how she held herself. She couldn't be sure, but she had a feeling that people could sense this different, lighter energy. Some people seemed to warm to her before she'd uttered a word. She still prepared persuasive ideas using what Mark had called the magic formula, but was amazed to find that even before this part of the meeting, people seemed to enjoy the conversation and to ask fewer difficult questions. It was as if, at a subconscious level, they could tell she was looking out for their interests, whether they decided to support the hospice or not. Which, of course, was exactly what she was doing.

Taken from Claire's notebook

HOW TO ASK FOR A LARGE GIFT –
my meeting with Olivia Waldron

So happy that OW has said she'd like to make a gift of £9000 to Alice House!

I'd been really worried because she wasn't able to come to Alice House, and in the end I had to go to her home on my own as Viv from the care team had flu.

But in spite of this, the meeting still went really well. Thank goodness for my trusty Story Bank.

As well as applying the five laws, I was really pleased that I managed to handle the actual moment of asking for money confidently. Mark's recent blog on three steps to an easier ask made it far less nerve-wracking than I'd feared. Here are the three steps I had not previously known about:

A) CONFIRM QUESTION. At the point in the conversation where it's appropriate to ask the donor to consider a gift, (ie after using the law of contrast about a topic you have found they care about), use a confirm question - a 'yes' or 'no' question. If they say 'no', you still have work to do before any request for a gift should be made. Find out what objections you need to re-frame. If they say 'yes', it will now be easier to ask, following on from their 'yes'. See part 6 in the conversation summary below, for the confirm question I used today.

B) SEPARATE INTO TWO. Never ask for the details of what a gift would pay for at the same time as asking them to consider whether in principle they'd like to make a gift. Ask in principle first. See part 8 below.

C) IT'S ABOUT VALUE, NOT PRICE. With a major gift, never, ever, ever ask for money!! Offer someone the chance to do something they care about...which happens to cost a certain amount. See part 9 below.

SUMMARY OF THE KEY STAGES OF OUR CONVERSATION WORTH £9000

1) Set my intention. I got really clear that I was not here to 'get' anything, but to help OW enjoy the meeting and if appropriate, offer her the opportunity to make a difference to people who will need day

hospice care next year.

2) Deliberately practiced confident, cheerful focus and body language on the way. As a result, I really was in a good mood by the time I got to her house, which helped me enjoy the meeting from the start.

3) Didn't spill my tea (!) and felt like I did okay at staying present and building rapport during the early chit chat bit.

4) As I had done on the phone, I mentioned early on that one purpose of the meeting was to share a funding opportunity with her. And was relieved that she was then happy to do a lot of the talking, in particular about her impressions of her visit to Alice House last month.

5) Asked if she'd like to hear a bit more about our day hospice unit. Managed to apply the law of contrast. Key problem — too many people end up unnecessarily going into hospital or other residential care away from their home, and that wrench can make them far more un-well. Included story about Joan. Showed the day hospice unit works in several ways, including by referring to both Sandra and Nigel, users of the unit who she'd met on her visit. They

relish being able to still live at home thanks to the weekly one-day visits to the day hospice. Also mentioned how pleased the Robertson Trust were with the impact their funding has had.

6) Asked confirm question, along the lines of '... from what you've said, my sense is you feel the unit makes a big difference. Have I understood you correctly?'

7) Thank goodness, all the signals she had sent up to now proved accurate. She said the unit is clearly vital for enabling people to stay at home for longer.

8) Asked if she would consider making a gift to help us run the unit over the coming year. She said, 'I'm not sure, just how much are we talking?'

9) Said that to provide top quality care for a patient in Sandra's condition for one day a week, costs around £750 per month. And would she consider enabling us to do that for a year, which would cost £9000.

10) She had three or four new questions at this point, which I handled. In the end she said I should send her a short proposal, but she was certain

she'd like to do her bit to support the unit. The only question she has is how soon she'll be able to release funds. I said that some donors decide to split their gift into quarterly or monthly instalments, which she said would suit her. After checking the proposal, she will put in writing how she would like to spread her gift.

PHEW!! I know they won't always be as straight forward as this, but equally I'm sure the techniques I've been practicing helped make the meeting far more smooth than it would have been six months ago. Am loving my job right now!

• THE FIFTH LAW •
THE LAW OF
STATE

—

THE GREATEST FACTOR IN OUR ABILITY TO INFLUENCE IS OUR STATE

—

CHAPTER 11

Petrified

'What a bloody nightmare,' Claire muttered to herself. The exercise machine was set at level 8 and she was running much faster than normal.

Since meeting Mark and Laura in October, and hearing about the law of state, Claire had become increasingly interested in the relationship between body and emotion. After reading a couple of books and several interesting blogs about health, she had come to the conclusion that there was a far closer link between the two than she had been brought up to believe. And so she had gradually started taking better care of herself. She had become more conscious of what she ate, which mostly meant more vegetables and salads in addition to whatever else she would normally have had.

But perhaps the biggest change was a return to regular exercise. She hadn't gone crazy. But she had started going to the gym or for a swim once a week and she had got back into badminton with her friend Reka. Claire had really enjoyed playing at university but somehow, once she moved to London it had seemed too much bother. But since January they'd been going every Tuesday and wondered why they'd ever stopped.

The other difference was just a bit more walking every day. For months she had been getting up fifteen minutes earlier so that she could walk to Finsbury Park tube instead of getting the bus, and she found the difference this tiny change made to her energy levels was undeniable. Claire had always fervently believed that she was not a morning person (she'd read a long time ago that either you were or you weren't), but by starting with a brisk walk she found she got to the office energised and ready to tackle her most important, lucrative tasks at the start of the day. She found this gave her a positive momentum for the rest of the day.

But at this moment Claire's state was pretty far from okay. She had gone straight to the gym after work. She had now been running hard for nearly twenty minutes; her cheeks were pink and her hair was sweat-damp.

In the mirror she saw the guy on the next machine glance her way. She wondered if her angry muttering had been audible above the music. She grabbed her towel and marched to the other side of the gym to use the rowing machine.

Actually, the exercise had made her feel a bit better. She no longer felt completely paralysed with fear, and she could at least think straight. And, as she considered her options, she realised that a call to Mark might help.

It was seven months since he and Laura had introduced her to the fifth law and she hadn't seen him since. He was with his children when he called, but he offered to talk the problem through the following morning.

She called him and explained her predicament. Her former manager, Joanna, had last October submitted a proposal to speak at the Fundraising Conference in July. It had been accepted in January, but by then she had left Alice House and gone travelling abroad.

Unable to make contact with Joanna, the conference organisers had called Claire's director to ask if someone else from Alice House would be willing to present. If not, they said they could cancel, but with six weeks till the conference they said they'd rather not lose the session unless they had to.

'So what did you tell her?'

'I said I'd think about it. They've agreed it would be okay to tweak the title so I could talk about the strategies that have helped me raise more money this year. And my director really wants me to do it, because this sort of thing helps put Alice House on the map, so it will be easier to recruit good fundraisers in the future. She told me the decision is completely up to me, but I don't really feel I've got much choice. What do you think I should do?'

'Well you've got some great examples from your success this year that would really help other fundraisers. It's perfect timing. But it doesn't matter what I think, does it Claire?'

Several seconds went by. 'Well, I know I *should* do it, in spite of being petrified of doing presentations. I guess I'm going to have to say "yes", aren't I?'

'Excellent news,' said Mark. 'You'll do a great job.'

Claire wasn't so sure. 'Hmm. Thanks.' Talking to donors and presenting in small internal meetings was one thing, but setting herself up to hold the attention of a hundred of her peers, many of whom would be far more experienced than her, felt like *mission impossible*.

'Any tips, Mark?'

'Only this – have a think about the five laws of fundraising persuasion, which you have so far used to help your supporters. But this time apply them in relation to the fundraisers who will come to your conference session. They are now the audience you should use the five laws to help.'

'I'm not sure I follow. How will I do that?'

'I'm confident you'll work it out, Claire. I'll meet you to run through it if you like, but only after you've given it some thought. Good luck.'

Mark clearly had nothing to add, so Claire thanked him and hung up.

> '...think about the five laws of fundraising persuasion, which you have so far used to help your supporters. But this time apply them in relation to the fundraisers who will come to your conference session.'

Three weeks later

They were again sitting in one of Mark's training rooms.

'Okay, so I'm going to call the session *The fourth law – the law of contrast.'*

Mark nodded. 'Intriguing title. Good start.'

Then Claire explained what she planned to say. Inspired by the law of firepower, she had decided to tell as many specific examples from her conversations with companies and donors as she could, to help her audience with ways they could find and use stories in their work. Mark made a few comments as she ran through the talk.

When she'd finished, she asked 'Do you think it's alright?'

'No, Claire, it's not alright ... this content is in fact excellent'

Mark shook his head. 'No. No, Claire, it's not alright ... this content is in fact excellent.' He seemed genuinely impressed. Claire had worked really hard to bring each of the ideas to life with tangible examples, and on paper it was shaping up to be a really useful session.

There was so much great content, Mark's main suggestion was to cut down the number of ideas she planned to cover.

'This is really useful, thanks. But truth be told, I'm still petrified when I think about actually doing it. I'm scared, the same as when I called you the other day. I'm so scared of messing up in front of all those people. What can I do?'

'Okay, as I see it, you have designed a great presentation because you have applied the first four laws to persuading this audience. You made a decision to create a really useful presentation; you sought insight into who they are likely to be; you collected way, way, way more specific fundraising stories than any normal speaker ever does, and you have given the presentation an elegant structure so as to maximise the contrast between the problems fundraisers face and the results that applying your ideas can achieve.'

'Now, the one thing I think may need more work, is the fifth law.'

'I'll say. Whenever I think of standing up in front of all those people, I feel dreadful. I'm scared stiff ... and I can't stand feeling frightened like this.'

Mark stood up and walked to the window. He looked at her. 'Well, come on.'

She stood up and followed. Mark was looking up at an aeroplane trail, high in the clear blue sky. 'Well, okay, how would you *like* to feel?'

This was a silly question. 'What?'

'Well, it's just that during both our conversations about this presentation, you've told me several times that you get scared stiff or petrified, which is how you *don't* want to feel. My question is: how *do* you want to feel?'

'Errr. I take your point.' She took a calmer breath. 'I want to feel in control.'

'In control, great. Anything else?'

'Yes, I want to feel in control, and

'Whenever I think of standing up in front of all those people, I feel dreadful. I'm scared stiff ... and I can't stand feeling frightened like this.'

... able to handle everything, and maybe a little excited too. I really am excited to be sharing these techniques because they've helped me so much and I know they can help other people too.'

Mark smiled. His posture was as upright and open as ever, and Claire found herself standing the same way. She smiled as she realised that undeniably she felt a bit calmer than she had been two minutes earlier.

'Now how do you feel?'

'Errr, maybe a six out of ten now. I mean, I'm still worried about it, but just now I was feeling pretty dreadful about it, say level three or four. And I don't feel so bad now.'

'Okay, well since you want to feel calm and in control, let's carry on breathing in a way that might help you feel that way.' He smiled, and they both became more conscious of taking deeper, calm breaths.

'So, the first thing about conference sessions is that content is king. You need to have valuable ideas to share, ideally wrapped up in stories

'You need to have valuable ideas to share, ideally wrapped up in stories that help people understand them.'

that help people understand them. The good news is you've got that. Then the second thing, and the real secret to presentations that are not only valuable to your audience but which you genuinely enjoy giving, lies in the law of state. You told me you already feel better. Which bits of this law could we thank for your feelings changing from level three or four to level six?'

'Well, the biggest shift was how I changed my physiology. Just now I was looking down and I kept fidgeting and my breathing was fast and quite shallow. And now,' she stood up even straighter, and reluctantly forced a smile onto her face, 'I reckon Amy Cuddy would be proud of me, because already there is probably more poise-boosting testosterone and less stressy cortisol coursing through my veins.' She also felt a bit less serious now.

Mark nodded and then the familiar quizzical look played across his face. 'Still only at level six? I hope you weren't telling untruths because, to be honest, you look closer to an eight now.'

Claire narrowed her eyes. Was he doing his jedi mind tricks on her? Or was it that standing this way, being playful about the whole idea and talking about testosterone, really had freed her from the downward spiral she usually felt when she thought about public speaking?

'Okay, I feel more like a six and a half for the moment,' she admitted. 'So this is a start. And I do appreciate it. But this is the easy part. How am I going to do this in front of an audience?'

'Well, I'll show you a couple of other techniques, including the golden rule of confident presenting, but I'm getting a bit tired. If we sit down again, do you promise to sit in such a way that you keep that poise-enhancing testosterone flowing?'

'I promise.'

'Well, okay.' They sat down.

'So if the idea of making this presentation makes you nervous sometimes, what is it about presenting that makes you feel that?'

'What? Well, I'm worried that I'll forget what to say half way through, and that I'll look like an idiot. I'm quite worried I'll say something that'll show Alice House in a bad light. And mostly I'm worried that I'll be found out. I mean, I'm really not that special, all I've done is get some good ideas for what to do from you and then work hard.'

Mark was looking amused rather than sympathetic.

'If you want to feel confident and in control, and even a bit excited when you present, here are the things to remember. Firstly, find a better meaning for the act of presenting at the conference. And secondly, focus completely on helping your audience, rather than on protecting your ego.

'So, in terms of what this presentation currently means to you, from what you've said, my guess is that to you, presentations are a forum where experts with brilliant, original ideas can be held up to scrutiny; and they are situations in which mistakes are unacceptable, and to be avoided at all costs; and you feel you need to show you are good enough to be entitled to be up there.

'If you want to feel confident and in control, and even a bit excited when you present, here are the things to remember.'

'Now, you may say that these meanings are accurate representations of what we as a society link to conference presentations. But in fact there is no single correct meaning for what a presentation is. The truth is, everyone makes up their own meanings and believes them to be right.

'Did I ever tell you a really helpful definition I've borrowed from Tony Robbins as to what a belief is? He says "it's something you're

'Tony Robbins says "a belief is something you're certain of … but which may or may not be true"'

certain of … but which may or may not be true".

'If this makes sense to you, I invite you to think about adopting two more empowering meanings to believe about presentations that I have noticed the truly outstanding presenters believe. Since noticing how useful these beliefs are, I've found a way to believe them myself. The first is that a presentation is, at its purest, "a chance to share some ideas that may help my audience" and the second is "every presentation is a fantastic chance to learn more about presenting, which will in turn help me speak even more effectively, and help more people next time". Can you see how someone who believed these two ideas would act very differently, before, during and after their talk, than someone who had believed those other things.'

Claire thought it through. She did see that these ideas reduced the pressure on her having to know everything and perform perfectly, because it was no longer about her, it was about helping other people and where possible, learning. Neither of these meanings had featured much in the many hours she had spent obsessing about the presentation up to this point.

Claire realised that most of her worries had at some level been linked to a desire not to screw up and look stupid. But she still wanted to understand the second half of the golden rule, which he'd said was about focus. She asked Mark how she could change what she was focusing on.

'Well, what did you do to improve your confidence with donors?' he asked.

'Errr, well I learned how to ask myself a question that would help and not hinder me during that donor meeting or phone call.'

'So, what might be a useful question to ask, both as you prepare the presentation, and in the build up to going on stage?'

She looked blank.

Mark added, 'You're allowed to cheat and just tweak the question that helped your approach to donors.'

'Oh. Well, how about ... "How can I use this presentation to help as many people as I possibly can?"'

'Now you're talking!' Mark's face lit up. 'That will do very nicely. And here's another one that one of my coaching clients used: "How can I possibly help as many people as I can today, through what I say and how I say it, so that they get good ideas and make decisions to go and raise more money and make the world a better place?"'

'Hmmm. If that question was genuinely your focus as you got up to speak, I guess it would help. But it's such a mouthful. I'm not sure I could remember that, let alone ask myself it. Do you think mine will work?'

'Yes, I think it will work extremely well, as long as you say it to yourself *as if you mean it*. And even if the words are not perfect, it's a whole lot more useful to say this than all those other nonsense questions you were imagining answers to, about messing up and looking stupid.'

'You mean that if I deliberately ask myself this question, it can crowd out the voice in my head that normally imagines the worst?'

'That, Claire, is exactly what I'm saying. You don't even have to do this perfectly for it to interrupt the pattern of unhelpfully directed focus about protecting your ego. And let's get crystal clear about this. What you focus on is what you feel.'

> 'And even if the words are not perfect, it's a whole lot more useful to say this than all those other nonsense questions you were imagining answers to, about messing up and looking stupid.'

'But it's so different from what I'd normally say. It feels risky. Do you really think it will make a difference?'

'Well, it seems to me you have nothing to lose if it's any improvement on what you've been doing up till now. I agree it may be unfamiliar but how well was your old way of preparing working for you?

'I suppose the other thing I could tell you is that this technique is the reason I've secured the highest audience evaluation rankings at the UK Conference for Fundraising, at which more than seventy-five speakers speak ... more times than any other speaker. You might say that's because at my ripe old age, I should have clocked up some good feedback on occasion. But even early in my speaking career I was achieving feedback that my sessions were much more helpful than other people's. That's because my whole performance was guided by the desire to help the people who were in front of me. Claire, I'm not saying this to impress you. I am saying it to impress upon you that this tactic works. If you say these helpful questions to yourself enough times and say them as if you really mean them, your subconscious mind cannot fail to get the message, and then channel your energy, your thoughts and words, and the tone of your voice even, to enable you to help your audience. And a happy by-product of focusing on helping other people is increased confidence.'

'And a happy by-product of focusing on helping other people is increased confidence.'

On the tube back to work, Claire wrote detailed notes about what Mark had showed her. She shook her head as she realised that everything he had said was really what she already knew about changing your state when meeting supporters. She was surprised to discover that so much of what enabled expert presenters to speak successfully stemmed from how strongly they focussed on helping their audience. And while she still had to do the hard work of applying these techniques, she was relieved to know exactly what she had to practise.

CHAPTER 12

Devil's advocate

Claire paused for a moment and took a long drink from her water glass.

She was near the end of the presentation and had asked the audience if they had any questions. The water was a relief to her dry throat.

She looked out into the almost-full room and guessed there were seventy or eighty people. She forced herself to note that not only had no one fallen asleep, but almost all of them had seemed genuinely interested in what she had to say.

Not that it had all been plain sailing. She had started really well, but then lost her concentration when a couple of people had arrived ten minutes late. What distracted Claire was the way they had walked in. Claire knew that at some point in her life she must have arrived late to public gatherings like this, but when it did happen she would have taken care to cause minimal disturbance. Whereas one of these two late-comers, the man with the floppy hair and goatee beard, had still been on his mobile as he opened the door, so that the whole room heard him saying 'Yup, gotta go now mate, gotta go, bye.' He'd flipped his mobile shut with a flourish and sauntered to the back row where his colleague had found seats.

What had thrown Claire was not so much the interruption but the sense that he did not give a damn. In her world this behaviour did not compute. Claire knew such people existed. She'd watched The Apprentice enough times to see some characters with values pretty different from her own. And she had even learned how to handle donors with big egos, with varying degrees of success. But what sort of fundraiser is so taken by their sense of self-importance that they are unaware of their impact on eighty other people?

> What had thrown Claire was not so much the interruption but the sense that he did not give a damn.

Still, she had got back on track after that, mustering her concentration as she told the story of how she and her chief executive had won the pitch for Alice House to be chosen as her local department store's charity of the year.

But then Goatee had started to whisper and snigger. She'd managed to block him out for most of the talk but as it continued and the conference volunteer who should have been at the back of the room had disappeared, she became increasingly distracted. A couple of times she had not explained her ideas nearly as well as she would have liked. But her overall content was still strong and her time was nearly up, and so now she decided to finish by taking a last couple of questions.

'Are there any questions?'

There was a pause. Then from the back row Claire saw a hand raised.

'Yup, actually, I have a question.'

Claire felt sick.

Goatee had stood up. Even at this distance he looked unusually tall in his navy blue pinstriped suit. He looked like a City banker. And suddenly Claire knew that she recognised this man. He'd been clean shaven then, and the new goatee made his face look longer. She realised that he was the smug presenter whose session had been so short on practical information exactly twelve months ago. But now that he was on his feet and looking down his nose at her, that sense of self-importance was unmistakable.

'Hugo Mallam ... The International Council for Humanitarian Relief. Yes, so I've been working in this field for a little over seventeen years ... and for the sake of balance I'd like to offer these good people,' he gestured around him, 'a different point of view if that's alright. Because you know, in my seventeen years in this game, I've found that using case studies and the pulling-on-the-heart-string style of messaging works okay for some people ... but – tell me if I'm wrong – you seem to be suggesting a one-size-fits-all approach. And I know that some donors, especially women, are more emotional and I think your approach would probably work for many of them, when logic may be less important. But in my experience over seventeen years, this fluffy stuff just isn't of interest to some people, like the serious businessmen that we larger charities deal with. That's it. I just wanted to humbly offer this alternative viewpoint, to the one-size-fits-all approach you've shared.'

Claire didn't know how long the silence lasted. Probably only two or three seconds, but they were grindingly slow. She knew the colour had flushed to her cheeks like a chemical reaction. Had he not been listening to a single thing she'd said? Was he being sexist to rattle her, or was his understanding of human nature and gender differences genuinely this lazy? She knew she had left some things out, but had she explained her ideas this badly?

> Fleetingly, Claire had the impression that to him this really was some kind of competition, and as alpha male he knew he had regained control of the room.

Claire could feel all the eyes of the room on her. She heard herself saying 'Forgive me, errr, Hugo, you said you had a question. What's your question?'

He made a strange noise, somehow reminiscent of Kenneth Williams, in mock surprise. 'Oooh, well, I thought I'd made myself clear. The fact is, some donors don't go for heart-string-tugging case study stuff, they want facts. So maybe this fluffy cause-led approach would work fine sometimes, but since you insist, my question is: do you find that your strategy fails with serious business people?'

Goatee was trying to look sincere but he was failing to hide an air of triumph. Fleetingly, Claire had the impression that to him this really was some kind of competition, and as alpha male he knew he had regained control of the room.

She could feel the hot, prickly sensation of a crimson flush blotching angrily from her chest towards her neck.

Her mind raced. Her newly confident identity and all vestiges of self-respect were sinking into a heavy, familiar emptiness.

She was short of breath and yet, in the fragility she felt at that moment, she instinctively remembered the plucky essence of what she had learned from Amy Cuddy's TED talk, and it gave her something to grab onto. She steadied herself and then willed a deeper than usual breath into her lungs, and stood up straighter, led by her sternum. As she also willed herself to stand taller and take up more space, she felt the rush of some feisty survival instinct that meant 'You play the bully if you need to, but I will *not* play the victim'.

'I agree that many donors don't like or bother reading case studies. Frankly, neither do I … even though I'm a woman.' There was raucous, spontaneous laughter from the audience, who were delighted to hear Mallam being put in his place. Receiving a big laugh was a novel sensation that felt uncomfortable. But it gave her time to notice for the first time that most of the room was with her, and also to re-notice that Mark's friend James was sitting at the end of the front row. He caught her eye and made the small fist-pump gesture that tennis players do after hitting a winner.

Her voice a little stronger now, she continued, '… It's not for me to question what has or hasn't worked for you during your seventeen years. All I can say is, in achieving the modest success I've had this year, I've held a belief that seems to be different to yours. Namely, that every human decision of any importance is determined chiefly by feelings. Clearly logic often plays an important part, but I believe that all important decisions are made after we feel something. Certainly

She could feel the hot, prickly sensation of a crimson flush blotching angrily from her chest towards her neck.

the feeling is usually justified with logic. But without a feeling of some kind, the decision would not happen.'

Mallam was shaking his head, 'That's just not true, throughout my long and not unsuccessful career I can honestly say …'

As he spoke, stirred by the look she had had from James, Claire found herself smiling as if this were a game, and she had taken a small but undeniable step towards the audience as she held up her left hand. Few in the audience noticed the step, but most sensed a palpable shift in the energy Claire was projecting.

A further advantage she held was the microphone on her lapel. She cut in, 'Now Hugo, you had your say, and I listened.' She was managing to remain polite, but there was a little more steel in her voice now. 'You had your say, and I listened to your point of view. And I presume the reason you asked your question was that you wanted to hear my answer …' She paused for just long enough. Hugh's face was a picture more of surprise than annoyance. Even in banter with his rugby mates, he'd found that people usually back down if you go for their weaknesses hard and early. He hadn't expected this misinformed twenty-something girl to stand her ground and come back at him. Instinctively he knew that she had the upper hand and he would lose more face to press on.

'… As I say, until I studied some of the research in the fields of psychology and behavioural economics, I had the view that we largely rule our lives through rational thought. But my experience over the last year is that I had been misunderstanding some of the fundamentals that shape the

A further advantage she held was the microphone on her lapel. She cut in, 'Now Hugo, you had your say, and I listened.' She was managing to remain polite, but there was a little more steel in her voice now decisions people make. What I now know is that I can help people make decisions that are both in their interests and in favour of our charity, if I set out to evoke the right feelings. And one of the best ways to do that is to use specific examples about human beings. In other words, to tell specific, relevant stories.

'Maybe the best way I can answer is to tell you about Guinness at Alice House.'

Claire paused for a moment and looked at the rest of the audience, who she realised she had a chance to help.

'One of the things that some of our patients love about our hospice is that, famously, our bar trolley opens every day at eleven in the morning. For many people, having a drink is a way of enjoying themselves and the very fact that at our hospice you're allowed to carry on doing something you associate with good times and friends, and that you were probably denied in hospital, is a powerful signal that you're here to focus on living not dying. Creating the best possible quality of life in all senses of that word, not just medically, is immensely important at Alice House.

'About six months ago, we had a patient in his late sixties called Alf, who had cancer. He was very unwell and had a month or two to live. And Alf told us that almost every day of his adult life, his one daily treat had been to enjoy a pint of draught Guinness in his local. He wasn't a big drinker, but that was his little luxury. Well, he said he was happy enough drinking the Guinness that Margery poured out for him from the can on the drinks trolley. But Margery could tell that Guinness from a can wasn't quite the same as the real thing.

'So every day, for as long as he was well enough to keep drinking, Margery used to pop out to The Three Fishes down the road and buy him a pint of draught Guinness. And it got to be that the locals were so touched that they'd have arguments over who got to buy Alf's Guinness. Margery told me that Alf was made up, every day ... I think it really wasn't so much because of the Guinness, but because of how special it made him feel.'

Claire paused again. Then, smiling as a fresh memory struck her, 'and, I was sharing this story at an event with this really serious guy Graham. He's a partner at this big law firm. What he especially loved about the story was the last detail, which is that after a week or two a couple of the older locals wanted to meet this famous Alf who was drinking the Guinness they were sending, so from then until he died, several times a week they would pop in and visit Alf. I told Graham that the sight of the three of them sitting in our garden room enjoying their pints together sums up how great the hospice care environment can be.

'So then Graham, the serious, hard-nosed lawyer, told me the story struck a chord with him partly because it reminded him of his own father. But to be honest, and this is why I'm telling you this, I don't think the story of Alf's Guinness was the only reason his firm has decided to make us their charity partner for the next two years, which is a deal that's going to be worth £150,000. I mean, he said it was a thing which helped him personally to decide, but he said a key reason he got his fellow partners to agree was the stories I had told him about how our adoption by the Williams Martyn accountancy firm had reduced late payment of fees by 23% and how the number of hits on Heaney's estate agent website had increased by 11% during the month when they were sponsoring our summer fun run. And unless you're rubbish at selling houses, an increase of 11% into an estate agent's pipeline equates to more house viewings and more house sales at the end of the month ... which is probably why Heaney's have already extended their sponsorship to next year's fun run and Mud Challenge as well.

'... So if your question, Hugo, is "should we take a one-size fits all approach to each supporter?", as I said earlier, in case anyone got distracted during that part of my talk, my answer is absolutely not. What we say in every conversation and pitch must be adapted to who we're talking to. And if your question is "do I believe that systematically gathering and practising a range of persuasive things

'...that's why Graham's law firm, who have for the last nine years run a formal pitch process to choose their charity partner, decided to scrap that process and just adopt Alice House'

you could say, including stories about your cause and social proof stories about benefit to our partners?" In my experience, yes, it is absolutely worth deliberately preparing your capacity to be persuasive in this way.

'And in my view that's why Graham's law firm, who have for the last nine years run a formal pitch process to choose their charity partner, this year decided to scrap that process and just adopt Alice House without all that extra work ... because they really, really, wanted to become our partner.'

For most of her explanation Claire had been concentrating so hard on what she was saying and was so inspired by the ideas that flowed through her that she had not even managed to focus on individual people in the audience, as she knew you were supposed to. After she finished, she had dared to look back to where Mallam was sitting, but he had not met her gaze.

The room was silent. And suddenly Claire felt empty.

Something at the back of the room caught her attention. The volunteer, now miraculously back, was waving a piece of paper at her. She couldn't understand why.

The volunteer cleared his throat. 'Ladies and gentleman, before you go, could you please remember to fill in your feedback forms?'

And now Claire's feelings changed from empty to uncomfortable. Everyone was busying themselves with their form-filling. She was in no-man's land – her part in proceedings had ended, but she felt stranded. She desperately wanted to escape. After all the drama, all the adrenaline and testosterone and cortisol that had carried her along, she now felt more self-conscious than ever. Especially as it was so quiet. Trying to comprehend the awestruck silence, her mind churned with all the things she'd missed out and messed up that had resulted in Goat Face missing the point. Not only that, but she'd told the Guinness story a bit wrong, and also had not been able to remember the names of the two pub regulars.

Increasingly angry with herself, she grabbed her glass of water and drained it. As she started to put the glass down, she knew that the movement was too quick, out of control. The tumbler collided with the rim of the jug.

For a split second, the clang of glass on glass vibrated through the room.

Aghast, Claire looked down to discover the jug had chipped and a crack stretched down the side. A rivulet of water was snaking down onto the table and the floor. After all the stress, unable to hold her emotion in check any longer, it was almost a relief as she swore quietly to herself. Normally, no one would have heard. But her lapel mike was still on, and the ugly word carried with shameful clarity across the room.

CHAPTER 13

Presenter's remorse

James had been delighted with Claire's performance. It had not been the most relaxing sixty minutes of his life, and he had once even considered telling the idiot with the floppy hair to shut up. Was the man drunk? But he'd decided not to intervene as Claire was holding her own. And to witness her speak with such composure and passion at the end had been exhilarating, like watching his team score at the end of a cup tie.

But the feeling didn't last long as he saw the smash, heard the whispered swear word, and saw her recoil in embarrassment. Her usual cheerful energy had been crowded out by a frosty, tight-lipped mask. Fidgeting frantically, she was getting more and more anxious.

He moved quickly to the front and poured the remaining water from the leaking jug into the spare speakers' glasses. From his bag he gave her a packet of tissues to mop up the water while he gathered her notes.

'Anything else you need?' he asked.

'No, that's everything.'

'Great. Now I'd say you've earned us some lunch. It's usually sea-bass with rice on day 2.'

They followed the crowd up the stairs and through the main lobby. He heard a guffaw of laughter from twenty yards ahead and noticed Hugo Mallam's head above the crowd. Claire saw it too.

'Actually James, I'm not hungry. I can't stay here. I just need to get away.'

James considered dissuading her, but she was close to tears. He thought better of it.

'Sure, let's get out of here.'

They walked through the revolving doors into the too-bright July sunshine and crossed the street. Finding an Italian café, they sought out the furthest corner and sat down.

He looked her in the eye. 'Congratulations Claire. Your talk was brilliant, seriously brilliant. And the way you finished … I've never seen anything like it.'

'Thanks James ... thanks, but right now I feel empty. And I can only think of everything I messed up.'

James paused, over-riding his desire to just tell her she was wrong. He knew it would do no good unless he first understood and appreciated what was going on from her point of view.

After ordering coffee and sandwiches, he turned back to her.

'You said you feel you messed some things up ...'

'Yeah. There were all sorts of things I missed out, that if I'd explained them properly from the start people would have understood what I meant. I of all people know that you don't take a one-size-fits-all approach to talking to supporters. I really wanted to get that across. Everything I've learned this year is about knowing enough persuasive content that whatever you manage to gain insight from your donor about, you'll be able to respond in ways that are interesting to *them,* so that you help them understand that your charity deals with things that are important to them.'

Claire had not said a word since they had left the hotel lobby, but now the words came in a torrent. Her voice was charged with anger and disappointment but James was relieved that the protective mask was gone. He continued to listen as she vented all the ways she'd messed up. She told him that when Goat Face had sauntered arrogantly in and proceeded to whisper loudly to his mates, it had completely thrown her. *He was so rude.* And come to think of it, where the hell had the room volunteer been? Shouldn't he police this sort of thing? And she vented about the final Q and A, and how she wished she had handled it all differently.

James had barely spoken in ten minutes, but on the whole he had managed to stay present and listen to Claire's frustration. She had slowed down, and he dared to think the chance for her to let rip had helped.

'Sorry,' she said. 'I'm just so pissed off with the whole thing. I wish I'd never agreed to it in the first place.'

'Okay.' He finished his mouthful. 'Well, for what it's worth, I'm really pleased you agreed to do it. I appreciate you may not be able to agree with me right now. But truthfully, even with the bits you may wish you had done better, your presentation was more interesting – and here's the most important thing – *more useful to your audience,* than 95% of the presentations I've seen here over the years' – and he leaned in – 'and it was your first one!'

'But was it really any good? James, I appreciate you trying to cheer me up and everything, and I want to believe you, but the truth is I just can't. To me, everything just feels crap.'

James gave her a strange look. He was weighing something up. 'Could I tell you a story?' he said.

Claire smiled in spite of everything. 'Sure.'

'I'm not sure if he ever mentioned this, but I once worked quite closely with Mark. In fact, for three years I worked with him in the training department at Stand Up for Children. In the very early days my huge enthusiasm for helping people learn was not equalled by my then limited skills and experience as a trainer. And, to help me improve, Mark used to sit in on my sessions so he could give me feedback at the end.

'Well, I remember the first full day training session I ever led on my own.' A look of utter

> 'James, I appreciate you trying to cheer me up and everything, and I want to believe you, but the truth is I just can't. To me, everything just feels crap.'

'As the adrenaline subsides, you often get a massive low, as most actors and comedians coming off stage will tell you.'

embarrassment crossed his face. Claire could tell he didn't relish this memory. 'Ouch … Imagine presenting to and training twenty people for seven hours, and not a single activity or explanation goes like you want it to. And some bits go very badly.

'So, I did my best and toughed it out to the end of the day, and then sat down with Mark to get his feedback. And the biggest thing he taught me that day was the concept of *presenter's remorse* and most importantly, how you overcome it. You can guess what *presenter's remorse* is?'

'Tell me.'

'It's to do with the meaning element of the law of state. The human brain behaves strangely at the best of times, but none more so than directly after giving a presentation. As the adrenaline subsides, you often get a massive low, as most actors and comedians coming off stage will tell you. In that moment, unless you're careful, your brain can act like a heat-seeking missile to hunt down anything and everything that it deems was less than perfect in your talk. The result of this, if you give it free rein, is you leave with a completely skewed perception of the quality of what you presented. And this happens even without being barracked by a floppy haired idiot and a bit of bad luck with a water jug.'

She nodded. It made sense in theory.

'So how do you stop presenter's remorse? I feel so dreadful. How do you change your focus and change the meaning you feel?'

'Well, Mark would probably say that changing what you're doing with your body would do no harm, even if you don't feel like it.' He sat up straighter and smiled. She really didn't want to, but she did her best to pull herself out of her slouch. She still felt pretty miserable.

154

'The key thing Mark had me do after every single presentation, pitch or training I did, and I still do it to this day, is to sit down as soon as possible after the talk and ask myself two questions: "What am I pleased with (or if that's too hard, what *could* I be pleased with, if I really wanted to be?) And, secondly, what would I do differently next time?"'

'Okay … so it's a way of deliberately controlling your focus, and searching for other meanings that will help you overcome presenter's remorse.'

'That's right.'

'But do you have to do them in that order?'

'Nothing's compulsory and, believe me, when I first started doing this, I often would have sworn there was nothing in the whole presentation that I could feel pleased with, so I always wanted to skip to things that needed improving. But if you want to learn more quickly, have a happier life and make a bigger difference to people you care about, I advise you to do them in this order even *if you don't want to.*'

'But why? I really can't think of anything that went well.'

'Because you can either be a slave to presenter's remorse and feel unnecessarily rubbish most times you speak, or you can decide to train your mind to search for the good stuff, till it starts to do that automatically. What you focus on, you feel. And the more determinedly you search for some things to be pleased about, the quicker you'll find and feel that better meaning. Which is not to say you ignore what went badly, if such things exist. Of course, you want to be honest about those and make them better. But if you first

'But if you first notice what went well, then where there are improvements to make, you'll be in a far better state to think clearly and make those things better next time.'

notice what went well, then where there are improvements to make, you'll be in a far better state to think clearly and make those things better next time.

'Come on, I'll help you.' James was paying the bill. 'It'll probably be easier if we do it while walking – as you well know, the quickest way to change emotion is through motion.'

They left the café. As they walked they took it in turns to ask each other for things that Claire could be pleased about from the session or that had probably been valuable to the audience. James helped her see that in this game you can give yourself a point for even really basic things that some people might get wrong: 'you started on time'; 'your opening sentence was warm and confident'; 'I think my posture was upright and smiley for most of the time'. She thought some of these were too obvious and basic to matter, but nevertheless, she did start to remember more and more things that she realised had not been disastrous.

She was especially pleased with the laugh she got when responding to Mallam's comment about women being illogical. And she remembered that her efforts to make her slides much simpler and more visual had really helped because the audience were paying attention to her, not reading the slides.

James often asked her what it was about each point that she was pleased with, which was initially strange, but when she tried to explain why, she found that it did help her access positive feelings, rather than merely acknowledge the concept intellectually.

After ten minutes they had moved on to what Claire had called the cock-ups, and which James wryly re-phrased as 'things you'd want to do differently next time.'

By the time they'd walked for twenty minutes Claire was feeling a whole lot better. She had still not shaken off some inner fury about the confrontation with Mallam and the humiliation of swearing into the microphone. The memory stung like crazy. She was so upset that by smashing the jug and then swearing she'd made herself appear unhinged to eighty people from all the major charities in the country, all of whom would tell all their colleagues.

James had done his best to help her change her view of what had happened. She hadn't come across as unhinged; everyone could tell it was an accident. Not only that, but the entire audience was on her side anyway and would have happily sworn at Goat Face given the chance.

Intellectually she could see that some of what he said was true. But why did she still feel so upset?

They said their goodbyes and James headed back to the conference. Claire got on the tube to head for home.

On the way, she wrote down all the ideas they'd just talked about, which helped get them out of her head. Then she tried to distract herself by reading the novel from her bag.

———————

The next week was hard. Two of Claire's team were away, and the energy was suddenly different, more subdued. And they were all having to work hard to cover.

A week had passed and sometimes Claire felt a hollow ache in her chest. It went away when she was really busy, but when her brain wasn't occupied she found her mind wandering back to what happened at the conference. Even though she knew it couldn't help to keep going back over it, she found herself drawn again and again to reliving the most intense moments.

She did, however, find a few things helped her. Re-reading one of the books Mark had recommended earlier in the year, Life's Lessons from History's Heroes, she had found a quote which he had underlined in red pen. It was right at the end of the last chapter. There was something about it that seemed to resonate, so she copied it into her notebook:

'The credit belongs to the man who is actually in the arena, whose face is marred by dust and sweat and blood; who strives valiantly; who errs and comes short again and again, who knows the great enthusiasms, the great devotions, and spends himself in a worthy cause; and who, at the worst, if he fails, at least fails while daring greatly, so that his place shall never be with those cold and timid souls who know neither victory nor defeat.'

Theodore Roosevelt, 'Citizen in a Republic', April 23, 1910.

It was late on a Monday afternoon that Claire received not one, but two emails with titles that caught her attention. The first was from one of the conference organisers. Apparently she had compiled the feedback from all the forms submitted. Claire felt sick. And yet she was compelled to open the document straight away.

'The average score for speakers this year was 3.7 out of 5 for content and 3.8 out of 5 for presentation style.

'I am pleased to tell you that your session scored 4.4 for content and 4.1 for presentation style and your scores mean that you were one of our Top Twenty speakers for this year's conference.'

The document also contained the comments people had written on their feedback forms. Reading through these was also generally very positive. She couldn't see any really negative ones of the type that Hugo Mallam might have written. Perhaps he'd been in too much of a hurry to get to lunch. Perhaps he couldn't write?

The other email bore the intriguing title of *Game Changer*.

Dear Claire,

I hope you don't mind me contacting you out of the blue. I attended your talk at the conference a couple of weeks ago. It helped me so much and I've been meaning to write to thank you, but today I had such good news that I can't put it off any longer.

For one thing, in terms of the specific techniques you outlined for preparing what to say that would be persuasive … the timing was perfect, as last week I had a meeting with an important donor who had supported us years ago but who we'd lost touch with. Before the meeting I went through the whole of the Magic Formula you talked about, and came up with some really strong things to say about the two topics most likely to interest him. I especially made sure I found ways to bring to life just what is so difficult for our service users, as well as a couple of really strong stories of what a difference we have made for them. I had thought we didn't really have impact stories like that, because that's what my colleagues have always said, but like you said, the more you search, sure enough, you find they were there all along. All it took was an extra conversation with the right person from our programme staff.

The meeting went like a dream! The law of contrast and using specific stories to bring it to life had an extraordinary effect. The lucky part for us is that he had sold his business earlier in the year and had been getting a bit bored. He said our meeting helped him realise our charity is something exciting he can put his energy into again. He asked me to put together a proposal for £350,000! I delivered this to him on Friday and he called me back this afternoon to confirm that, yes, he will give us the money in two instalments split across the next two years. Not only that, but he'd like another conversation about getting more involved in some other way ("to help unlock other funds"). He's so fired up I can't believe it.

Secondly, I took so much from seeing you stand up to that silly man who had clearly not listened to a word you'd actually been saying. Between you and me, I think he couldn't bear the idea that if you're right, he's been under-prepared and under-achieving for his whole career. He's clearly got a massive ego, and that ego would fight tooth and nail rather than have to re-evaluate his whole career. Sometimes people go to any lengths to avoid being honest with themselves. Anyway, I could tell it wasn't easy for you standing up to him … but I think that's why the whole thing had such an impact on me. I kept thinking about it afterwards. It wasn't easy and you did it anyway and in the end the whole room was so pleased that you had made your point so eloquently – I really wanted to congratulate you at the end but saw that by that stage you just wanted to get away.

Anyway, I've been having quite a difficult situation at work recently and since seeing what you did, I've decided to stand up for myself more deliberately. I watched that Amy Cuddy talk on YouTube that you mentioned as well, and even just since making the decision to not play along with my colleague's game, I feel different, more confident somehow. And by forcing myself to actually do the posture things Amy explains, I think it's already changed how I feel.

And thirdly, since your talk I've also decided to stay in fundraising. I had been pretty unhappy for a while because despite all my hard work, I kept missing my financial target, and I was sick of feeling like a failure. But I've changed my mind and have decided to refocus my efforts on becoming more skilful at my job. You helped me see that focusing your effort and working hard at a few very specific skill areas does pay off. I now realise there are several things I can do, because that's basically what you said you've done to turn your results around.

I know this is cheeky, because people must ask for your help all the time, but I wondered if you'd let me buy you coffee so I can find out in more depth some things other than what you call the fourth law, that would help my skills and confidence to improve.

Best wishes,
Fiona Dawson
Major Gift and Partnerships Officer

As Claire read and re-read what Fiona had written, tears of relief rolled down her cheeks. Everyone else had gone home, and she was happy to let them flow.

She emailed Fiona back, congratulating her on her success and offering a couple of times she would happily meet for coffee the following week.

Next, she forwarded both emails to James, changing the title of the first to 'Thanks so much James!' and the second to 'Presenter's remorse no more'.

Then she turned off her computer, got her coat from the peg and locked the office. On the way down the stairs, she pulled out her mobile and found Mark's number. She figured this was a story he'd want to hear.

The FIVE laws of persuasion that transform your results

· THE FIRST LAW ·
THE LAW OF
DECISION

—

IN FUNDRAISING,
AS IN LIFE,
ALL GREAT PROGRESS
STARTS WITH
A DECISION

—

• THE SECOND LAW •
THE LAW OF
UNDERSTANDING
—

IF YOU WANT TO
INFLUENCE SOMEONE,
FIRST UNDERSTAND
AND APPRECIATE
THEIR WORLD

—

• THE THIRD LAW •
THE LAW OF
FIREPOWER
—

THE FUNDRAISER
WHO COLLECTS,
PRACTISES AND KNOWS
MORE STORIES WILL
FIND IT EASIER TO
INFLUENCE WHEN
IN CONVERSATION
WITH POTENTIAL
SUPPORTERS

—

• THE FOURTH LAW •
THE LAW OF
CONTRAST
—

THE MOST CERTAIN
WAY TO HELP SOMEONE
WANT TO GIVE IS TO
EVOKE A PROBLEM
THEY CARE ABOUT
AND THEN HELP THEM
BELIEVE YOUR CHARITY
IS ABLE TO SOLVE IT.

—

• THE FIFTH LAW •
THE LAW OF
STATE
—

THE GREATEST FACTOR
IN OUR ABILITY TO
INFLUENCE IS OUR
STATE

—

Claim your **FREE** fundraising materials

If you would like more help as you continue your journey, you can claim your bonus fundraising resources, worth more than £7.95 at

www.brightspotfundraising.co.uk/book-free-gift/

● Your online copy of **Pitch to Win**, *40 powerful tips to help you win more corporate partnerships for your charity*.
(Normal price £7.95)

● Your copy of **The Fundraiser's Meeting Checklist**, a tool which, like Claire, Rob's coaching clients have used to transform their results with donors, supporters and corporates (ordinarily not for sale).

Increased fundraising income following Rob's courses

To find out whether the Major Gift Mastery Programme or Corporate Partnerships Mastery Programme could transform your results too, go to www.brightspotfundraising.co.uk/training.

'I used the techniques I learned on Rob's course to double the number of memberships I sign up every month. These fundraising strategies are really powerful'.

SARAH JAYNE O'NEILL, MAJOR DONOR MANAGER, *STONEWALL*

'Rob showed my corporate fundraising team lots of excellent new business strategies. The techniques made a made a MASSIVE difference to our financial results, including helping to win a partnership worth £2 million'.

JESS COOMBS, HEAD OF CORPORATE FUNDRAISING, *TEENAGE CANCER TRUST* AND FORMERLY AT *ACTION FOR CHILDREN*

'Rob is without doubt the best fundraising trainer I have ever worked with. Years after attending his sessions I still use what he taught me, in fact, his strategies helped me win a partnership worth £4.5 million. If you can possibly get on one of his corporate fundraising courses, don't hesitate, because it will help you raise a lot more money'.

CIARAN BIGGINS, DIRECTOR, *MINDFOOD* AND FORMERLY NEW BUSINESS MANAGER AT *SCOPE* AND *TEENAGE CANCER TRUST*.

'As a Director of Fundraising I'm always looking for the very best, so I've used Rob's fundraising training every year for the last six years. His pitching and new business strategies are phenomenal and just as importantly, he lifts your team's confidence so that they go and apply it.'
ANDY HARRIS, DIRECTOR OF FUNDRAISING AND COMMUNICATIONS, *BREAST CANCER CARE*

'I've just heard from a well-known London brand that they've chosen our charity to be their new partner, worth around £250,000. In fact, they were so keen to choose us that they scrapped the final round (staff vote), to award us the partnership just hours after we pitched. I can think of at least three specific strategies that I took straight from Rob's course that helped us win this partnership so emphatically. I really don't think we'd have won without Rob's advice!'
TORI GRIFFITHS, SENIOR PARTNERSHIPS MANAGER, REBUILDING CHILDHOODS APPEAL, *NSPCC*

'Following the course, Major Gift Fundraisers at the NSPCC increased gift income by 29%'.
CITATION BY *UK SKILLS NATIONAL TRAINING AWARD*

'Following Rob's course I became way more focussed and applied his techniques for securing meetings with High Net Worth individuals. As a result, in one week I persuaded 56 very wealthy and influential people to meet me. All of the meetings have gone incredibly well and some have agreed to support us financially. So if you want to raise a lot more money, get yourself a place on Rob's programme'.
LOIS A WOOLFE, HEAD OF DEVELOPMENT, *NATIONAL LIBRARY OF SCOTLAND*

'Days after attending Rob Woods' training, I used the strategies he teaches on powerful stories and the structuring gift requests in a donor meeting. It was one of my best moments in fundraising. I felt in control of the meeting and the donor willingly agreed to make a gift of £100,000 to our Emergency Appeal. I find Rob's sessions are a vital way to help me and my team continue to improve our fundraising skills.

MARK ROWLAND, HEAD OF FUNDRAISING, *VSO*

'Rob trained our team who were phoning clergy and as a result 5000 churches agreed to a face to face meeting. He also trained our fundraisers for those meetings, and they've achieved a fantastic 65% success rate, which means 3,250 churches have agreed to fundraise for us during Christian Aid Week. I'm very clear that Rob's outstanding training helps you raise more money'.

CATHERINE LOY, HEAD OF CHRISTIAN AID WEEK, *CHRISTIAN AID*

'I was on the pitch team to win a partnership worth £1,000,000. I was determined to pitch to the best of my ability. Rob helped me present with confidence, persuasiveness and enthusiasm, enabling me to connect with the pitch panel – and we won the partnership.

KIRSTY LAWSON, CORPORATE ACCOUNT TEAM MANAGER, (HEAD OF) AT *ALZHEIMER'S SOCIETY*

"Before going on Rob's course, I hadn't booked any meetings with donors. Following the training - which was fantastic - I got on the phone and booked 10 meetings for the next two months. The meetings resulted in 5 gifts worth a total of £55,000. I absolutely recommend you go on his training"

POLLY BISHOP, MAJOR GIFTS OFFICER, *CHRISTIAN AID*

'I was delighted with the course that Rob did for my corporate team. We've recently secured three new partnerships worth around a million pounds each, and what we learned with Rob helped inform our approach to building these partnerships.'

AMIT AGGARWAL, HEAD OF CORPORATE PARTNERSHIPS, *BRITISH HEART FOUNDATION*

Rob's exceptional training has taken our programme to the next level. One example was a colleague re-connecting with a lapsed donor on the phone, resulting in a £100k+ gift; his first in four years. I would absolutely recommend Rob's training programme as an invaluable investment for any fundraising team.

VICTORIA STEPHENSON, HEAD OF MAJOR DONORS, *UNICEF UK*

'Rob's training helped our team raise more money and hit our target of £1.25 million, which is why I would recommend his major gift master-classes to anyone. One strategy alone caused me to act differently and generated a new gift worth £62,000. If you get a chance, do this training because IT WORKS'.

TOM HALL, DIRECTOR OF PHILANTHROPY, *SCOPE*, WINNERS OF THE IOF AWARD FOR BEST USE OF MAJOR GIFT FUNDRAISING, 2013.

'We recently had a pitch we just had to win. I'm absolutely clear that what we learned from Rob helped us get the deal, which is a partnership that's going to raise £1 million. Rob is better at helping you influence your donor to get the gift than anyone I've met.'

BEN SWART, HEAD OF STRATEGIC AND COMMERCIAL PARTNERSHIPS, *NSPCC*

'I've found the Corporate Partnerships Mastery Programme hugely helpful already. It's helped me in so many ways, but as an example, I applied one of Rob's pitching techniques and it completely wowed the panel, and has resulted in a partnership worth over £100,000.'

KIERAN CORNWALL, SENIOR STRATEGIC PARTNERSHIPS MANAGER, *CYSTIC FIBROSIS TRUST*

To find out whether the Major Gift Mastery Programme or Corporate Partnerships Mastery Programme could transform your results too, go to www.brightspotfundraising.co.uk/training.

My guarantee – 'I'm so certain you'll love these programmes, if you're not already delighted by the end of Day 1, you can have all of your money back, and keep the first CD as my gift.' Rob Woods

I have found the following books and resources helpful on the subjects covered in this book.

- *Awaken the giant within*, Anthony Robbins
- *Influence, science and practice*, Robert Cialdini.
- *Life's lessons from histories heroes*, Michael Anthony Jackson
- *Made to Stick*, Chip and Dan Heath
- *Pitch anything*, Oren Klaff
- *The edge* (audio pack), Anthony Robbins
- *The elements of persuasion*, Richard Maxwell and Robert Dickman
- *The jelly effect*, Andy Bounds
- *The go giver*, Bob Burg and Jon Mann
- *The small BIG*, Robert Cialdini, Steve Martin, Noah Goldstein
- *Storytelling can change the world*, Ken Burnett
- *Unleash the power within* (live seminar), Anthony Robbins
- *Your body language shapes who you are*, (www.TED.com), Amy Cuddy

Made in the USA
Middletown, DE
27 April 2022

64857194R00097